THE ULTIMATE
WASHINGTON CAPITALS
TRIVIA BOOK

A Collection of Amazing Trivia Quizzes
and Fun Facts for Die-Hard Capitals Fans!

Ray Walker

Exclusive Free Book

Crazy Sports Stories

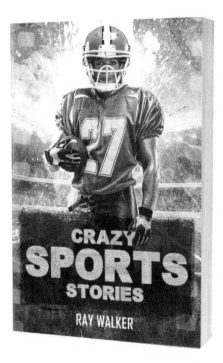

As a thank you for getting a copy of this book I would like to offer you a free copy of my book Crazy Sports Stories which comes packed with interesting stories from your favorite sports such as Football, Hockey, Baseball, Basketball and more.

Grab your free copy over at

RayWalkerMedia.com/Bonus

CONTENTS

INTRODUCTION

Hockey fans are often inspired by what they see on the ice, and their favorite team is typically a source of excitement, loyalty, and pride. Fans belong to a community of others who all experience the same emotions while following their on-ice heroes.

Washington Capitals fans are part of this community as they wear the red, white, and blue of the Capitals' uniform with pride. The Capitals have been entertaining the masses for close to half a century with a multitude of memorable moments. Washington has iced some of the game's greatest players and coaches over the years, with plenty of joy and drama to go along with them.

This Capitals trivia book is a celebration of the franchise through all of its ups and downs. It takes a look back at what makes this club so unique by reminding fans of all the critical moments of its history.

Each chapter is meant to entertain and test your knowledge of the Capitals organization from day one to the present. Each of the fifteen chapters consists of twenty multiple-choice and true or false quiz questions, as well as the all-important answers on a separate page. The chapters also contain ten "Did You Know" facts about the franchise.

Some fans will read the book as a way of testing their knowledge about the Capitals' history, while others will look forward to learning something new or entertaining themselves.

Of course, due to the competitive nature of sports, there are sure to be readers who will challenge their fellow Capitals fans to see who has the most knowledge about the club, or who simply has the best memory.

So, whether you're reading the book for entertainment purposes, as a learning or teaching experience, reliving the past, or challenging others, you'll be sure to strengthen the bond with your favorite NHL team along the way.

The statistics and information gathered for the book are up to date as of the beginning of 2020. The Capitals will surely add some more fascinating history to the team over the coming years, but this book will fill you with enough knowledge to become an up-to-date expert.

CHAPTER 1:

ORIGINS & HISTORY

QUIZ TIME!

1. In which season did the Washington Capitals make their NHL debut?

    a. 1967-68
    b. 1970-71
    c. 1974-75
    d. 1979-80

2. The Washington Capitals play their home games in the American state of Washington.

    a. True
    b. False

3. Which other expansion franchise joined the NHL in the same season as the Capitals?

    a. Buffalo Sabres
    b. Vancouver Canucks
    c. Kansas City Scouts
    d. Edmonton Oilers

4. The new franchise was named the Capitals because it is based close to Washington, D.C., the capital of the United States of America.

    a. True

    b. False

5. The Capitals' home arena from 1974 to 1997 was named the Capital Center.

    a. True

    b. False

6. Washington moved to a new home arena in 1997.

    a. True

    b. False

7. Who was the first owner of the Capitals franchise? He also owned the Washington Bullets NBA club.

    a. Harold Ballard

    b. Milt Schmidt

    c. Abe Pollin

    d. Ted Leonsis

8. Who was the first general manager of the Capitals?

    a. David Poile

    b. Milt Schmidt

    c. Max McNab

    d. Jim Anderson

9. Who was the first player, and 1st pick overall, ever chosen by Washington in the NHL Entry Draft?

a. Defenseman Greg Joly

b. Left winger Paul Nicholson

c. Left winger Mike Marson

d. Center Brian Kinsella

10. Washington was beaten 6-3 in New York by the Rangers in their first-ever NHL contest. The team's first win was a 4-3 home conquest over which squad?

a. Minnesota North Stars

b. Los Angeles Kings

c. Boston Bruins

d. Chicago Blackhawks

11. During their inaugural season, the Capitals posted the worst winning percentage in NHL history. What was it?

a. .075

b. .131

c. .250

d. .333

12. The Capitals managed to win just one of 40 road games in their debut NHL season.

a. True

b. False

13. The Capitals played 80 regular-season games in their first campaign and posted how many victories?

a. 6

b. 8

c. 10

d. 12

14. Which player led Washington in goals, assists, and points in the team's inaugural big-league season?

    a. Right winger Tommy Williams
    b. Left winger Denis Dupere
    c. Center Ron Lalonde
    d. Defenseman Gord Smit

15. The Capitals made their first Stanley Cup playoff appearance in 1982-83 and were eliminated in the 1st round three games to one by which team?

    a. Toronto Maple Leafs
    b. Pittsburgh Penguins
    c. Philadelphia Flyers
    d. New York Islanders

16. The Capitals didn't win their first playoff series until 1983-84 when they beat which team in three straight games?

    a. Montreal Canadiens
    b. Philadelphia Flyers
    c. New York Rangers
    d. New York Islanders

17. Washington has won the Stanley Cup just once in the franchise's history.

    a. True
    b. False

18. How many head coaches have the Capitals had from the team's inception until the 2019-20 season?

a. 10

b. 16

c. 18

d. 21

19. Who was the first Washington player to be named to the NHL's First All-Star Team?

    a. Defenseman Rod Langway - 1982-83

    b. Defenseman Scott Stevens - 1987-88

    c. Goaltender Olaf Kolzig - 1999-2000

    d. Winger Alexander Ovechkin - 2005-06

20. Who was the first Capitals player to have his number retired by the franchise?

    a. Mike Gartner

    b. Dale Hunter

    c. Yvon Labre

    d. Rod Langway

QUIZ ANSWERS

1. C – 1974-75

2. B – False

3. C – Kansas City Scouts

4. A – True

5. A – True

6. A – True

7. C – Abe Pollin

8. B – Milt Schmidt

9. A – Defenseman Greg Joly

10. D – Chicago Blackhawks

11. B – .131

12. A – True

13. B – 8

14. A – Right winger Tommy Williams

15. D – New York Islanders

16. B – Philadelphia Flyers

17. A – True

18. C – 18

19. A – Defenseman Rod Langway - 1982-83

20. D – Rod Langway

DID YOU KNOW?

1. The Capitals franchise was awarded by the NHL in July of 1972. The team is currently owned by Ted Leonsis and the Monumental Sports and Entertainment Company, which he heads. Leonsis bought the club in 1999, and the Capitals work with two minor league affiliate teams, which are the South Carolina Stingrays of the East Coast Hockey League (ECHL) and the Hershey Bears of the American Hockey League (AHL).

2. The first head coach of the Capitals was Jim Anderson, a former NHL player who competed in seven games with the Los Angeles Kings. Anderson was fired by Washington midway through the team's inaugural season with a wins-losses-ties record of 4-45-5 after 54 games. He was replaced by George 'Red' Sullivan, who went 2-16-0 in 18 games in charge before being fired at the end of the season.

3. The Capitals' first NHL goal was scored by Jim Hrycuik on October 9, 1974, in the club's first regular-season outing, a 6-3 loss to the New York Rangers at Madison Square Garden. Hrycuik would go on to play just 21 career games in the NHL, all with Washington, and post five goals and five assists.

4. The Ottawa Senators' road record was an NHL all-time worst 1-41-0 in 1992-93. However, Washington also won

just one away game in their first NHL season, a 5-3 triumph over the California Golden Seals on March 28, 1975.

5. After missing the playoffs in their first eight NHL seasons, there were numerous rumors regarding the club's future in 1982. Some local fans and businesses started a campaign called 'Save the Caps' to keep ownership from moving the franchise elsewhere. David Poile was then hired as general manager, and his shrewd trades helped the team improve by 29 points in 1982-83 from the previous season. The club made the postseason for the first time in 1982-83 and to the delight of the fans stayed put.

6. Once the Capitals got a taste of playoff hockey in 1982-83, the club would then go on to reach the postseason for the next 13 consecutive seasons. Their best playoff finish during that stretch was reaching the 3rd round in 1989-90. Washington beat the New Jersey Devils four games to two in the 1st round. They then ousted the New York Rangers four games to one before losing in four straight to the Boston Bruins in the Conference Finals.

7. After missing the playoffs in 1996-97, the Capitals rebounded by reaching the Stanley Cup Final for the first time the next season. They beat Boston in five games in the opening round and followed up by eliminating the Ottawa Senators in five games and the Buffalo Sabres in six in the next two rounds. However, they ran into defending champion the Detroit Red Wings in the Final and were swept in four games.

8. The Capital One Arena is located in the Chinatown area of Washington, D.C. The Capitals' home rink was known as the MCI Center from 1997 to 2006 and the Verizon Center between 2006 and 2017. The building is also the home venue of the NBA's Washington Wizards and Georgetown University's men's basketball squad.

9. The first player ever drafted by the Capitals to be inducted into the Hockey Hall of Fame was winger Mike Gartner. He was chosen in 1979 with the 4th overall pick and inducted into the Hall of Fame in 2001. Gartner played 1,432 regular NHL season games with five different teams and notched 708 goals and 627 assists for 1,335 points. He also holds or shares four regular-season Capitals' scoring records and two NHL records.

10. Washington won the Stanley Cup for the first time in franchise history in 2017-18 when they downed the Vegas Golden Knights four games to one in the Final series. The Capitals beat the Columbus Blue Jackets in six games in the 1st round and eliminated the Pittsburgh Penguins in six in the 2nd round. They then reached the Final by edging the Tampa Bay Lightning in seven contests in the Eastern Conference Final.

CHAPTER 2:

JERSEYS & NUMBERS

QUIZ TIME!

1. How many Capitals players have had their jersey number retired?

    a. 0

    b. 4

    c. 7

    d. 9

2. The three predominant colors that make up Washington's current jersey are red, white, and blue.

    a. True

    b. False

3. No Capitals player has worn the number of former goaltender Olaf Kolzig since he retired in 2008. What number did Kolzig wear?

    a. 29

    b. 30

    c. 31

    d. 37

4. Hall of Fame winger Mike Gartner had his number retired by Washington in December of 2008. What number did he wear?

    a. 11
    b. 14
    c. 21
    d. 32

5. Capitals winger Alexander Ovechkin has made which number famous throughout his career, as his nickname also contains his jersey number?

    a. 7
    b. 8
    c. 18
    d. 28

6. Who has been the only Capitals player to ever wear the number 7, which has since been retired?

    a. Rod Langway
    b. Yvon Labre
    c. Dale Hunter
    d. Dennis Maruk

7. The Capitals and all other NHL teams have retired the number 99 in honor of Wayne Gretzky, the league's all-time leading scorer.

    a. True
    b. False

8. Washington and all other NHL teams have also retired number 66, which was made famous by Mario Lemieux.

a. True

b. False

9. The highest jersey number worn in Capitals history has been 96. Who wore it?

a. Nathan Walker

b. Jaromir Jagr

c. Milan Novy

d. Phil Housley

10. Hall of Fame forward Sergei Fedorov played a total of 70 regular-season games with Washington in 2007-08 and 2008-09. What number did he wear?

a. 12

b. 19

c. 44

d. 91

11. The Capitals' third jersey in the 2015-16 season was dark green in color.

a. True

b. False

12. Which famous Washington, D.C., landmark has been used as a logo on the Capitals' jersey?

a. The White House

b. The Lincoln Memorial

c. The National Mall

d. The Capitol Building

13. The Capitals have utilized a secondary logo of a bald eagle with its wings spread to represent the letter W. What is the nickname of the logo?

    a. Bald Bird
    b. Spread Eagle
    c. Weagle
    d. Beagle

14. The letter T in the Capitals' written jersey logo is replaced by the figure of a hockey stick.

    a. True
    b. False

15. In which season did Washington introduce a black alternate jersey?

    a. 1976-77
    b. 1981-82
    c. 1997-98
    d. 2018-19

16. The Capitals made a major uniform change in 1995-96 by incorporating which colors into their jerseys?

    a. Yellow and green
    b. Orange and black
    c. Gold and purple
    d. Blue and black

17. Former Washington captain Dale Hunter made which since-retired jersey number famous?

a. 17

b. 24

c. 32

d. 33

18. Who has been the only player to wear number 88 for the Capitals?

    a. Nate Schmidt

    b. Zach Sanford

    c. Jay Beagle

    d. Jose Theodore

19. What common symbol is featured above the Capitals' logo on the team's jerseys?

    a. Stars

    b. Stripes

    c. Crosses

    d. Hearts

20. Which Washington player has worn the C on his jersey since January 5, 2010?

    a. Tom Wilson

    b. Nicklas Backstrom

    c. T.J. Oshie

    d. Alexander Ovechkin

QUIZ ANSWERS

1. B – 4

2. A – True

3. D – 37

4. A – 11

5. B – 8

6. B – Yvon Labre

7. A – True

8. B – False

9. D – Phil Housley

10. D – 91

11. B – False

12. D – The Capitol Building

13. C – Weagle

14. A – True

15. C – 1997-98

16. D – Blue and black

17. C – 32

18. A – Nate Schmidt

19. A – Stars

20. D – Alexander Ovechkin

DID YOU KNOW?

1. Four Washington players have had their jersey numbers retired as of the 2019-20 season. Yvon Labre had his number 7 retired in 1980, while fellow defender Rod Langway's number 5 received the same honor in 1997. Center Dale Hunter's number 32 was hung from the rafters in 2000, and winger Mike Gartner's number 11 joined it in 2008.

2. Former Capitals goaltender Olaf Kolzig never had his number 37 retired officially. But as of the 2019-20 campaign, no other Washington player has worn it since Kolzig left the club in 2008. Kolzig played 711 of his 719 regular-season NHL games with the Capitals and currently owns or shares 13 club goaltending records.

3. When the Capitals entered the league in 1974, the team wore predominantly white home jerseys and red ones on the road. They also wore either red, white, or blue pants with the jerseys, but the white pants were discarded after several games when they evidently became see-through and discolored when wet.

4. The lowest jersey number worn by a Capitals player has been the number 1, which 13 different goaltenders have proudly displayed throughout franchise history. The highest jersey number worn has been 96, which was used by Hall of Fame defenseman Phil Housley in 1997 and 1998.

5. The most popular jerseys in team history have been the

numbers 23 and 25, which have each been worn by 26 different players. Number 28 has been worn by 24 players, while 23 different Capitals have worn the numbers 24 and 26.

6. Although the number 13 is regarded as bad luck by many superstitious people, a total of five different Washington players have worn the digit on their back. These have been Andrei Nikolishin, Bates Battaglia, Joey Tenute, Jiri Novotny, and Jakub Vrana.

7. The Capitals have tried several different designs and logos on their jerseys throughout the years, with the most common logo being the word "Capitals" written on the front of the sweater. They have also used a screaming eagle, a bald eagle, and a graphic of the Capitol Building in Washington, D.C.

8. The Capitals wore specially designed jerseys and uniforms for both the 2011 and 2015 NHL Winter Classic Games. They also wore special uniforms for the 2018 NHL Stadium Series Game, which was played outdoors at the U.S. Naval Academy close to Washington, D.C., in Annapolis, Maryland.

9. Washington made only minor changes to the team uniform and jersey in the first two decades of the club's existence. The first major change came in 1995 when the screaming eagle was introduced as the logo, and the jersey colors were changed from red, white, and blue to predominantly blue and white, with shades of bronze and

black thrown in. A third jersey, which was predominantly black, was brought in two years later. The blue-based road jerseys were retired in 2000 when the club reverted to red, white, and blue.

10. Throughout Washington franchise history, a total of 90 different jersey numbers have been worn by players. Every number from 1 to 70 has been worn by at least one player. No player has worn the number 71, but at least one player has worn each number from 72 to 96, with the exception of 73, 80, 86, 93, and 95.

CHAPTER 3:

FAMOUS QUOTES

QUIZ TIME!

1. Which Capitals player was quoted as saying, "What happens in Vegas stays in Vegas, but we brought the cup home!" during the team's 2018 championship parade?

    a. Alexander Ovechkin

    b. T.J. Oshie

    c. Tom Wilson

    d. Nicklas Backstrom

2. Before the 2017-18 season began, Alexander Ovechkin said these famous words in broken English, "We're not gonna be suck this year."

    a. True

    b. False

3. What year did Alexander Ovechkin say this to *The Sporting News* when asked about his legacy as a hockey player? "You want to be successful like every person, like hockey players in the past. I want to be like Michael Jordan, Kobe Bryant—the kind of people who won championships."

a. 2010

b. 2011

c. 2015

d. 2019

4. Which Capitals player was quoted as saying, "I am disappointed in the length of the suspension," after being banned for 21 games in the 1992-93 playoffs?

   a. Pat Elynuik

   b. Todd Krygier

   c. Dale Hunter

   d. Alan May

5. Which NHL team was Alexander Ovechkin referring to in October 2019 when he said, "They must play differently if they want to win a Stanley Cup."?

   a. San Jose Sharks

   b. Montreal Canadiens

   c. Toronto Maple Leafs

   d. Arizona Coyotes

6. After winning the Stanley Cup, which Caps player said, "It's unbelievable. We're going to be friends forever. And hopefully, in 20 years, we're going to be calling each other talking about this day."?

   a. Evgeny Kuznetsov

   b. Nicklas Backstrom

   c. Braden Holtby

   d. Jay Beagle

7. Wayne Gretzky once called the Capitals organization a "Mickey Mouse operation."

   a. True

   b. False

8. When former NHL goaltender Glenn Healy remarked in the book *Ice Wars*, "I was kind of afraid of him. He could beat you from 50 feet out, and he was deadly in closer," which Caps player was he talking about?

   a. Adam Oates

   b. Bobby Carpenter

   c. Mike Gartner

   d. Peter Bondra

9. Which Caps Hall of Fame player once said this about visiting the shrine as a youngster, "I went to the Hall of Fame with my dad. I can't say I really remember too much about it."?

   a. Rod Langway

   b. Larry Murphy

   c. Adam Oates

   d. Phil Housley

10. Which former Caps blueliner was former NHL coach Scotty Bowman speaking about when he stated, "He's the nearest thing to Bobby Orr I've seen."?

   a. Al Iafrate

   b. Kevin Hatcher

   c. Rick Green

   d. Phil Housley

11. "My speed is my greatest asset" was said by which Caps player?

    a. Mike Gartner

    b. Alexander Ovechkin

    c. Dino Ciccarelli

    d. Peter Bondra

12. Ulf Dahlen said this when leaving the Caps: "Obviously, I have a lot of memories here...but at the same time I'm going to put all my energies into moving forward and doing my best for the Thrashers."

    a. True

    b. False

13. Which former Washington player said this about rival Claude Lemieux of the Colorado Avalanche, "I can't believe I shook his frigging hand."?

    a. Larry Murphy

    b. Dave Shand

    c. Chris Simon

    d. Dino Ciccarelli

14. After allowing a fluky playoff goal in overtime, which former Caps goalie said, "That's one thing I can't do—stop someone who doesn't know what he's doing."?

    a. Mike Palmateer

    b. Roger Crozier

    c. Olaf Kolzig

    d. Craig Billington

15. When questioned about his knack for racking up assists, which Caps player stated, "Obviously, it means that I played with some players who were able to put the puck in the net."?

    a. Adam Oates
    b. Nicklas Backstrom
    c. Michal Pivonka
    d. Dmitri Mironov

16. Caps goalie Olaf Kolzig once said he'd like to represent South Africa in ice hockey at the Olympics.

    a. True
    b. False

17. Which Capitals coach said, "Emotion—a short term friend—can carry you a long way. What you need is a long-term companion like talent."

    a. Jim Schoenfeld
    b. Tom McVie
    c. Ron Wilson
    d. Terry Murray

18. When asked by reporters why he failed to shoot at the empty net when the opposing goalie was pulled, which Caps rearguard replied, "Empty net goals are for sissies."?

    a. Al Iafrate
    b. Ken Klee
    c. Joe Reekie
    d. Rob Zettler

19. When he was traded to the Capitals from Montreal, which player said this about the general manager who dealt him, "He just made the worst trade in the history of the NHL."?

    a. Brian Engblom

    b. Craig Laughlin

    c. Rod Langway

    d. Doug Jarvis

20. Former Caps winger Mike Gartner once said he'd like to play defense for a season with the club.

    a. True

    b. False

QUIZ ANSWERS

1. C – Tom Wilson

2. A – True

3. B – 2011

4. C – Dale Hunter

5. C – Toronto Maple Leafs

6. B – Nicklas Backstrom

7. B – False

8. C – Mike Gartner

9. C – Adam Oates

10. D – Phil Housley

11. D – Peter Bondra

12. B – False

13. D – Dino Ciccarelli

14. A – Mike Palmateer

15. C – Michal Pivonka

16. B – False

17. B – Tom McVie

18. A – Al Iafrate

19. C – Rod Langway

20. B – False

DID YOU KNOW?

1. After four years behind the Capitals' bench, former coach Barry Trotz left the club after winning the Stanley Cup and had this to say about the team the next season while coaching the New York Islanders in the playoffs: "The Capitals have virtually the same team. I know all that background with that group of guys, and I'm always going to have a very special bond with them because we climbed the mountain together."

2. After Alexander Ovechkin passed former Capitals player Peter Bondra to take over the franchise lead in points scored in 2014, Bondra had this to say: "I'm really happy for Alex. It's well deserved. I've been watching him since he came in his first year here. He's a really exciting player to watch, and it was a matter of time. From now on, he is going to re-write Caps history."

3. When asked about his views on fighting in the NHL, Washington captain Alexander Ovechkin stated, "Fighting is necessary in hockey. But if you fight, you have to choose your partner carefully. If you're an experienced player and you want to fight, you can't choose a player who has never fought in his life."

4. After Montreal, Quebec native Robert Picard was drafted by the Capitals in 1977, and he wasn't too happy with the situation. Picard was hoping to play with Quebec in the

World Hockey Association (WHA), but he had already signed a deal with the Caps. He then said, "I'd rather deliver pizzas in Quebec City than play hockey in Washington."

5. When Washington was suffering one of the worst seasons in NHL history in their first year in the league in 1974-75, head coach Jim Anderson stated to the press, "I'd rather find out my wife was cheating on me than keep losing like this. At least I could tell my wife to cut it out." Anderson was fired shortly after, as the team continued its losing ways.

6. Center Mikhail Grabovski's debut for the Capitals was quite impressive as he scored three goals and an assist. The feat came in the first game of the 2013-14 season, and it was the first time a Capitals player scored a hat trick on opening night. After the game, Caps teammate Brooks Laich praised Grabovski by saying, "He's a gritty guy who sticks his nose in there, and he's scored a lot of goals around the net. Happy for him that he's getting his offense going, and hope it continues." Grabovski finished his only season in Washington with 13 goals and 35 points in 58 games.

7. Forward T.J. Oshie told reporters after the Caps won the Stanley Cup that his father was suffering from Alzheimer's disease. Oshie added, "He doesn't remember a lot of stuff, but you bet that he's going to remember this game." Oshie posted 21 points during the 2017-18 postseason to help Washington capture their first championship.

8. When speaking of his Capitals Hall of Fame teammate Mike Gartner, fellow winger Craig Laughlin had this to say to the *Washington Post* newspaper: "There's no other player from our era that I remember who could come full speed down the right-wing and take a slap shot that was so hard, it was either going in or was going to kill the goalie." Gartner finished his career with 708 goals and was the first player to score 30-goal seasons with five different NHL clubs.

9. Center Adam Oates earned 1,079 assists in his NHL career to rank 8th on the all-time list. The Hall-of-Famer explained his habit of passing the puck so much by telling the media, "Growing up as a kid, my father was British and a soccer player. His idol was a guy that passed the ball a lot, Stanley Matthews. Our family thought if you could be unselfish, your teammates would always like you."

10. Peter Bondra was once quoted as saying this when explaining his role with the Capitals: "Two or three years ago, every game I want to score. After I score, I have a spark, and I'm so happy I want more. Now I'm kind of different. I'm not saying I lost my spark—I still have it—but I don't chase the goal as much as I used to. I'm playing for the team, and I still know I can score, but it's different than two or three years back. You have to play defense, that's how you win."

CHAPTER 4:

CATCHY NICKNAMES

QUIZ TIME!

1. The team nickname for the Washington Capitals is?

    a. The D.C.ers

    b. The Washers

    c. The Caps

    d. The Presidents

2. Capitals current tough-guy forward Tom Wilson is commonly known as "Whip."

    a. True

    b. False

3. What is the nickname of current Washington blueliner Dmitry Orlov of Russia?

    a. Tree

    b. Snarls

    c. Orly

    d. Dee

4. Former Washington forward Andre Burakovsky was known by which nickname before he was traded to the Colorado Avalanche?

    a. Burt
    b. Dr. Dre
    c. Burracuda
    d. Skis

5. The "Ice Cheetah" was the nickname of which former Washington forward?

    a. Jason Chimera
    b. Craig Laughlin
    c. Sergei Fedorov
    d. Mike Gartner

6. What is the nickname of current Capitals defender John Carlson?

    a. Carly
    b. Killer
    c. Jumbo
    d. JC

7. Former Washington center Michael Latta went by the nickname "Steam," which was shortened from "Steamboat."

    a. True
    b. False

8. When patrolling the blue line for Washington, defenseman Mike Green went by which nickname?

a. Green Day

b. Greener

c. Green Grass

d. Murph

9. Goaltender Don Beaupre had a couple of nicknames when playing with the Capitals. One was "Donnie Bo," and the other was?

a. Bo Prey

b. Bobo

c. Donny Boy

d. Dope

10. Former Washington star winger Peter Bondra, who retired with 503 NHL goals to his name, was commonly known as "Bonzai" with his other nickname being?

a. Peeper

b. The Special Agent

c. Peebo

d. The Bondsman

11. Defender Sergei Gonchar was often known as "Gonch" while skating with the Capitals, but he was also known by a second nickname. What was it?

a. Serge

b. Brad Pitt

c. Rocket

d. Benjamin Button

12. Defenseman Al Iafrate was known for his booming slap shot throughout his NHL career. He was most commonly

known as "Wild Thing," while his other nickname was "The Hammer."

   a. True

   b. False

13. Russian veteran forward Ilya Kovalchuk was acquired by the Capitals in late February 2020. He's often called "Kovy" by teammates, but what is his more creative nickname?

   a. The $103 Million Dollar Man

   b. The Man From UNCLE

   c. The Spy

   d. Kolchak the Night Stalker

14. Defensive stalwart Rod Langway was arguably the best Capitals defenseman ever. What was his nickname?

   a. The Boss

   b. Langway the Only Way

   c. The Secretary of Defense

   d. Hot Rod

15. Washington captain Alexander Ovechkin gave teammate Nic Dowd his nickname, which is named after a famous TV character. What is it?

   a. Kramer

   b. Maxwell Smart

   c. Inspector Gadget

   d. Judge Judy

16. Defenseman Scott Stevens was such a hard hitter during his career that the former Capitals star was known as "Captain Crunch."

a. True

b. False

17. "The Big Cheese" was the nickname of which former Capitals player?

a. Phil Housley

b. Joel Ward

c. Chris Brown

d. Mel Angelstad

18. Adam Oates was part of the famous "Hull and Oates" nickname when playing with Brett Hull. The nickname for the duo originated while playing with the Capitals.

a. True

b. False

19. Opposing fans often like to come up with derogatory nicknames for their rivals. What is one such nickname for the Capitals?

a. First Round Exit

b. Hapless Caps

c. Second Round Exit

d. One Hit Wonders

20. What is another nickname which has often been associated with the Washington Capitals?

a. The Barmy Army

b. The Red Army

c. Capital Punishment

d. The Washington Express

QUIZ ANSWERS

1. C – The Caps

2. A – True

3. B – Snarls

4. C – Burracuda

5. A – Jason Chimera

6. C – Jumbo

7. A – True

8. D – Murph

9. B – Bobo

10. B – The Special Agent

11. D – Benjamin Button

12. A – True

13. A – The $103 Million Dollar Man

14. C – The Secretary of Defense

15. D – Judge Judy

16. A – True

17. B – Joel Ward

18. B – False

19. C – Second Round Exit

20. B – The Red Army

DID YOU KNOW?

1. When the Capitals players attended a seminar by motivational speaker Tony Robbins in 2017, Robbins asked them to yell out the name of an animal or something spiritual. Center Lars Eller responded with "Tiger" and that his been his nickname ever since.

2. Washington's Russian winger Alexander Ovechkin is commonly known by a pair of nicknames. The franchise's all-time leading goalscorer wears the number 8 on his jersey and is known as the "Great Eight." He's also simply known as "Ovi" by many fans and teammates, while others like to call him "Alexander the Great."

3. Former Washington defenseman Brooks Orpik was known to teammates as "B&O Railways." Teammates gave the 6-foot-3-inch, 200 lb. Orpik the nickname because they said he had the ability to run opposing players over just like a freight train.

4. When Swedish forward Marcus Johansson played with the Capitals, he also went by two nicknames. The fans knew him as "MoJo" while former Capitals player Eric Fehr said his teammates preferred to call him "JoJo."

5. Veteran Washington center Nicklas Backstrom has been called several nicknames over the years, with monikers such as "Papa," "Dad," "Nicke," "Backy," "Star Lars," and "Nicklas Snackstrom." However, fans have come up with

several others, including "Nickleback-Strom" and "Back-to-Back Strom."

6. When Capitals netminder Braden Holtby played in the American Hockey League (AHL) with the Hershey Bears, he was soon known as "Ellen." He got the nickname because his hairstyle looked similar to that of television personality Ellen DeGeneres.

7. While Holtby may have been known as "Ellen" while playing with Hershey in the minors, he's been known by several nicknames in Washington. These include "Holtbae," "Holtbeast," "Holts," "The Beast," and "The Great Wall of Chinatown." He earned the last nickname since the Capitals play in the Chinatown area of Washington, D.C.

8. Blueliner Matt Niskanen was such a fan of the slap shot from the point while playing with Washington that his teammates started calling him "Niskannon." Niskanen, who was also known as "Tun," helped Washington win the Stanley Cup in 2017-18 but was traded to the Philadelphia Flyers for fellow defender Radko Gudas in June of 2019.

9. Former Capitals goalie Jim Carey played with the team when actor Jim Carrey was one of the hottest stars in Hollywood. Due to the same pronunciation of their names, Carey had to put up with nicknames based on the actor's famous movie roles. This resulted in monikers such as "Ace," "The Mask," and "The Net Detective."

10. Another Capitals goaltender who was known by several nicknames during his career was the great Olaf Kolzig of

South Africa. Kolzig was commonly known as "Zill," "Kolzilla," "Godzilla," "The O-Liminator," and "Olie the Goalie."

CHAPTER 5:

THE CAPTAIN CLASS

QUIZ TIME!

1. How many captains have the Capitals had since their inception?

   a. 10
   b. 12
   c. 14
   d. 15

2. The first Washington captain in the club's inaugural NHL season in 1974-75 was Yvon Labre.

   a. True
   b. False

3. Up until the 2019-20 season, the longest-serving captain in Washington's history has been?

   a. Doug Mohns
   b. Ryan Walter
   c. Rod Langway
   d. Alexander Ovechkin

4. Who was named captain of the club in January 2010?

   a. T.J. Oshie
   b. Nicklas Backstrom
   c. Alexander Ovechkin
   d. Tom Wilson

5. Which Washington captain was traded to the Columbus Blue Jackets in December 2009?

   a. Chris Clark
   b. Jeff Halpern
   c. Steve Konowalchuk
   d. Brendan Witt

6. Who was the first full-time defenseman to captain the Capitals?

   a. Kevin Hatcher
   b. Brendan Witt
   c. Rod Langway
   d. Yvon Labre

7. Chris Clark was the Capitals' captain when the team won the Stanley Cup.

   a. True
   b. False

8. Which Washington captain won the James Norris Trophy as the NHL's best defenseman in 1982-83 and 1983-84?

   a. Doug Mohns
   b. Brendan Witt
   c. Kevin Hatcher
   d. Rod Langway

9. How many Capitals captains have been named to the NHL's end-of-season First All-Star Team?

   a. 1
   b. 2
   c. 4
   d. 5

10. How many Washington skippers have won the Art Ross Trophy for leading the NHL in scoring for a season?

    a. 0
    b. 1
    c. 2
    d. 3

11. Which Washington forward captained the team in 1998-99 and failed to score a goal in his total of 50 games that season?

    a. Adam Oates
    b. Steve Konowalchuk
    c. Dale Hunter
    d. Chris Clark

12. The Capitals have played three NHL seasons without a team captain.

    a. True
    b. False

13. Which player was never a Washington captain?

    a. Bill Clement
    b. Guy Charron

c. Denis Dupere

d. Jeff Halpern

14. In terms of games played, which Washington captain wore the C for the shortest amount of time, a total of 46 games?

a. Bill Clement

b. Yvon Labre

c. Doug Mohns

d. Brendan Witt

15. How many total games did Ryan Walter miss in his three full seasons as Washington captain?

a. 0

b. 2

c. 10

d. 44

16. The Capitals have never named a goaltender as team captain.

a. True

b. False

17. How many Capitals captains reached the 30-goal mark at least once while wearing the C for the team?

a. 0

b. 1

c. 4

d. 8

18. Defenseman Scott Stevens was one of the greatest NHL captains in history; however, he never wore the C with Washington.

a. True

b. False

19. How many Washington captains failed to score at least one goal during a season in which they wore the C?

    a. 1

    b. 2

    c. 4

    d. 6

20. How old was high-scoring forward Adam Oates when named team captain in 1999-2000?

    a. 24

    b. 30

    c. 33

    d. 37

QUIZ ANSWERS

1. C – 14

2. B – False

3. C – Rod Langway

4. C – Alexander Ovechkin

5. A – Chris Clark

6. D – Yvon Labre

7. B – False

8. D – Rod Langway

9. B – 2

10. B – 1

11. C – Dale Hunter

12. B – False

13. C – Denis Dupere

14. A – Bill Clement

15. B – 2

16. A – True

17. C – 4

18. A – True

19. C – 4

20. D – 37

DID YOU KNOW?

1. Two former Capitals captains have been inducted into the Hockey Hall of Fame. These are defenseman Rod Langway and forward Adam Oates. As of 2019-20, Langway was the team's longest-serving skipper from 1982-83 to part way through the 1992-93 season, while Oates wore the C from 1999-2000 to 2000-01.

2. In the 2001-02 campaign, Washington didn't name a traditional captain as the team decided to go with two co-captains. These were left winger Steve Konowalchuk and defenseman Brendan Witt. The Capitals went back to the one captain system the next season when Konowalchuk wore the C by himself.

3. The youngest player to be named captain of the Capitals has been forward Ryan Walter, who was just 21 years old when given the honor in 1979-80. Walter would captain the squad for three full seasons. The oldest Washington captain was veteran Doug Mohns, who was 41 when Washington made their NHL debut in 1974-75.

4. The Capitals have named a total of five defensemen as team captain along with 10 forwards, even though the franchise has had just 14 captains. The reason for this is because the club's first captain Doug Mohns played both defense and forward.

5. Of the 14 different captains the Capitals have named

throughout history, just four of them were originally drafted by the club. These were Ryan Walter in 1978, Kevin Hatcher in 1984, Brendan Witt in 1993, and Alexander Ovechkin in 2004.

6. Alexander Ovechkin is the only Washington player to be drafted 1st overall who went on to be named team captain. Greg Joly was taken 1st overall in 1974, and Rick Green was the top pick in 1976. Ovechkin went 1st overall in 2004, while former captain Ryan Walter was drafted 2nd overall in 1978.

7. While some NHL teams prefer to name several alternate captains instead of a team captain, the Capitals aren't among them. Washington has had a captain for every NHL season the club has played. The only season the club didn't have a captain on the ice was in 2004-05 when the campaign was wiped out by a lockout. Steve Konowalchuk captained the team the season before the lockout for several games, and Jeff Halpern took over the year after.

8. While Rod Langway was captain of the Capitals for 10 full seasons and part of an eleventh, the Hall of Fame defenseman basically looked after his own end first and didn't worry about chipping in offensively. Langway went goalless in three of his seasons as captain and chipped in with just one goal on two occasions. In fact, between 1989-90 and 1992-93, he managed only one goal in three and a half seasons.

9. When Alexander Ovechkin was named Washington captain in January of 2010, he became the first European to

captain the team. At 24 years of age, he was also the Capitals' second youngest skipper behind Ryan Walter, who was 21 when given the honor. At the time in 2010, Ovechkin was also the third youngest skipper in the NHL.

10. The Capitals have also iced some excellent alternate captains throughout the franchise's history. These include future Hall-of-Famer Jaromir Jagr and Hall-of-Famers Sergei Fedorov, Mike Gartner, and Scott Stevens. Also included on the list are numerous other star players such as Nicklas Backstrom, T.J. Oshie, John Carlson, Sergei Gonchar, Peter Bondra, Michal Pivonka, and Joe Juneau.

CHAPTER 6:

STATISTICALLY SPEAKING

QUIZ TIME!

1. The Capitals' inaugural NHL season was one of the worst in league history. How many games did they win in 1974-75?

    a. 6
    b. 8
    c. 11
    d. 13

2. Former Capitals player Adam Oates earned the most assists in the NHL in both 2000-01 and 2001-02.

    a. True
    b. False

3. Which Capitals player led the team with 37 goals and 85 points in just his third season with the team?

    a. Mike Gartner
    b. Dino Ciccarelli
    c. Peter Bondra
    d. Alexander Ovechkin

4. Which Washington winger led the team in rookie scoring in 2006-07, with 22 points in 52 games?

    a. Alexander Semin
    b. Anson Carter
    c. Steve Eminger
    d. Boyd Gordon

5. Who was the first Washington player to notch 50 goals in a season?

    a. Mike Gartner
    b. Peter Bondra
    c. Dennis Maruk
    d. Alexander Ovechkin

6. The most shorthanded goals in a single season by a Washington player is?

    a. 5
    b. 6
    c. 8
    d. 11

7. Forward Bobby Carpenter scored 53 goals in 1984-85 for Washington.

    a. True
    b. False

8. The Capitals' record for the longest regular-season goal-scoring streak by a player is how many games?

    a. 5
    b. 9

c. 12

d. 15

9. Which Capitals player scored 30 goals as a rookie with the California Golden Seals in 1975-76?

   a. Bob Carpenter

   b. Dennis Maruk

   c. Ron Lalonde

   d. Jack Egers

10. Which Washington player led the team with 26 goals and 49 points in 1975-76?

   a. Hartland Monahan

   b. Tony White

   c. Ace Bailey

   d. Nelson Pyatt

11. Which Washington player led the team in scoring in 1974-75, with 22 goals and 58 points, and also had the worst plus/minus rating among forwards at -69?

   a. Mike Marson

   b. Mike Bloom

   c. Tommy Williams

   d. Bill Lesuk

12. Goaltender Ron Low won all eight of the Capitals' games in their first season in the NHL.

   a. True

   b. False

13. How many times were the Capitals shut out in the 1974-75 campaign?

a. 6

b. 10

c. 12

d. 17

14. How many Washington players skated in all 82 regular-season games in 2018-19?

    a. 0

    b. 2

    c. 7

    d. 12

15. How many games did backup goaltender Pheonix Copley play with Washington?

    a. 5

    b. 12

    c. 27

    d. 68

16. Right winger Mike Gartner holds the Capitals' record for the longest point-scoring streak at 17, which he achieved twice in his career.

    a. True

    b. False

17. Who led the Caps in playoff scoring with 32 points in 24 games when the team won the Stanley Cup in 2017-18?

    a. Alexander Ovechkin

    b. John Carlson

    c. T.J. Oshie

    d. Evgeny Kuznetsov

18. Heading into the 2019-20 season, the Capitals' all-time playoff record was?

    a. 135-147
    b. 100-182
    c. 147-135
    d. 141-141

19. Who coached Washington to a 39-32-11 record in 1995-96?

    a. Ron Wilson
    b. Jim Schoenfeld
    c. Terry Murray
    d. Tom McVie

20. Peter Bondra led the NHL in power-play goals in 2000-01 with 22 goals.

    a. True
    b. False

QUIZ ANSWERS

1. B – 8

2. A – True

3. C – Peter Bondra

4. A – Alexander Semin

5. C – Dennis Maruk

6. B – 6

7. A – True

8. B – 9

9. B – Dennis Maruk

10. D – Nelson Pyatt

11. C – Tommy Williams

12. A – True

13. C – 12

14. B – 2

15. C – 27

16. A – True

17. D – Evgeny Kuznetsov

18. A – 135-147

19. B – Jim Schoenfeld

20. A – True

DID YOU KNOW?

1. Forward Peter Bondra was drafted in the 8th round in 1990 at the age of 22. In February 1994, he scored five goals in a game against the Tampa Bay Lightning, with four of them coming in the first period. He then led the league with 34 goals in the 47-game 1994-95 season and led the league again with 52 goals in 1997-98, along with Teemu Selanne of Anaheim. Bondra also owns the team record with 32 career shorthanded goals.

2. The Capitals had a wins-losses-ties record of 8-67-5 in their first season in the league for a dismal 21 points. The team set several NHL records with the campaign at the time, including the fewest wins and points in a season. They also allowed a league-record 446 goals against and posted the worst goal difference by a team in one season at -265. Just one of their victories came on the road, which is also tied for the worst away mark in a season.

3. Bobby Carpenter was the first NHL player to be drafted right out of high school, and he earned an assist after just 12 seconds in his NHL debut in 1981. In 1984-85, Carpenter became the first American-born NHL player to record 50 goals when he tallied 53 goals and 45 assists. Carpenter would later win the Stanley Cup in 1994-95 with the New Jersey Devils.

4. Hall of Fame winger Mike Gartner scored at least 35 goals

in all eight of his full seasons with Washington and managed an even 50 in 1984-85 when he also posted 52 assists for 102 points. Gartner retired in 1998 and shares the record for the most consecutive 30-goal seasons with former Capital Jaromir Jagr and current Washington captain Alexander Ovechkin. Gartner also holds the NHL record for most 30-goal seasons at 17.

5. Capitals captain Alexander Ovechkin could possibly finish his career as the NHL's all-time goalscoring leader. He has tallied eight 50-goal seasons so far and has led or shared the league lead in goals on nine occasions. When the NHL paused in 2019-20 for the coronavirus pandemic, Ovechkin was the current active leader in goals with 706 and was ranked 8th in league history. His aim is to break Wayne Gretzky's record of 894 before he retires.

6. The Capitals have iced some of the NHL's top-scoring players over the years, and as of 2020, three of the league's top eight goalscorers had played for Washington. Jaromir Jagr ranks 3rd on the all-time goal list, with 766, while Mike Gartner's 708 goals rank him 7th overall, and Alexander Ovechkin's total of 706 place him 8th.

7. One of the top scorers in Washington history was center Dennis Maruk. He was the first Caps player to score 50 goals when he notched an even 50 in 1980-81. Maruk also led the team in assists that season with 47, as well as 97 points, 16 power-play goals, and five game-winners. He also shared the team lead for shorthanded goals with

Bengt Gustafsson as they tallied two each. He then scored 60 goals and 76 assists for a team record 136 points the next season.

8. When the Capitals took to the ice for the first time in the NHL in 1974-75, defenseman Bill Mikkelson was unfortunate enough to set a league record for the plus/minus statistic when he finished the campaign at -82. Mikkelson played 59 games and posted three goals and seven assists. Fellow blueliners Greg Joly and Gord Smith were -69 and -60, respectively, that season.

9. Olaf Kolzig played for the Capitals from his NHL debut in 1989-90 until 2007-08. He holds the team record for regular-season games by a goalie at 711. He also holds club marks for most wins at 301, most losses at 293, and most ties at 86. He allowed the most goals against at 1,860, recorded the most shutouts at 35, and scored the most points from the crease at 17. Kolzig's six playoff shutouts are also a team high.

10. When it comes to Capitals head coaches, Bryan Murray leads the franchise in regular-season games coached at 672, as well as most wins at 343 and the most points at 769. Murray also coached the team to a club-record 24 playoff wins in a record 53 playoff contests coached. Murray won the Jack Adams Award in 1984 as the NHL's coach of the year.

CHAPTER 7:

THE TRADE MARKET

QUIZ TIME!

1. Which Hall of Fame defenseman was traded to Washington from Montreal in 1982?

   a. Ray Bourque
   b. Paul Coffey
   c. Rod Langway
   d. Borje Salming

2. Langway would go on to win two James Norris Trophies with Washington as the NHL's best defenseman.

   a. True
   b. False

3. What did Washington give up to the Montreal Canadiens in 2020 to land forward Ilya Kovalchuk?

   a. Cash
   b. A 1st round draft pick
   c. A 3rd round draft pick
   d. Future considerations

4. Which team was forward Andre Burakovsky traded to in June of 2019?

   a. Montreal Canadiens
   b. Colorado Avalanche
   c. Calgary Flames
   d. Edmonton Oilers

5. Washington received a 2nd and a 3rd round draft pick from the New Jersey Devils for which forward in July 2017?

   a. Carl Hagelin
   b. Nic Dowd
   c. Eric Fehr
   d. Marcus Johansson

6. Who was acquired by Washington along with defenseman Kevin Shattenkirk in February 2017?

   a. Goaltender Pheonix Copley
   b. Forward Chris Bourque
   c. Forward Travis Boyd
   d. Defenseman Rick Green

7. Forward Lars Eller was acquired in 2010 from the Montreal Canadiens for two 2nd round draft picks.

   a. True
   b. False

8. What did the Capitals receive from the Colorado Avalanche for goaltender Semyon Varlamov in July 2011?

   a. A 1st round draft pick
   b. A 1st and 2nd round draft pick

c. Two 2nd round draft picks

d. A 2nd and 3rd round draft pick

9. 9. When defenseman Sergei Gonchar was dealt to the Boston Bruins, Washington received Shaone Morrisonn as well as a 1st and 2nd round draft pick in 2004. Who did they select with the 1st round pick, which was 27th overall?

a. Mikhail Yunkov

b. Patrick McNeil

c. Francois Bouchard

d. Jeff Schultz

10. Which team gave Washington a 1st round draft pick and Jiri Novotny for Dainius Zubrus and Timo Helbling at the trade deadline in 2007?

a. Detroit Red Wings

b. Arizona Coyotes

c. Buffalo Sabres

d. Anaheim Ducks

11. Which Capitals general manager acquired forward Daniel Winnik in a trade with the Toronto Maple Leafs?

a. Brian MacLellan

b. George McPhee

c. David Poile

d. Max McNab

12. Washington acquired defenseman Tim Gleason from the Carolina Hurricanes at the 2015 trade deadline.

a. True

b. False

13. The last trade George McPhee made as general manager of the Capitals in April 2014 saw him acquire a conditional 7th round draft pick from the Nashville Predators. Who did Washington give up?

    a. John Mitchell
    b. Martin Erat
    c. Garrett Stafford
    d. Jaynen Rissling

14. General manager Milt Schmidt made the first trade in Washington history in 1974 by giving up cash to the Calgary Flames for which future captain of the team?

    a. Bill Clement
    b. Yvon Labre
    c. Ryan Walter
    d. Doug Mohns

15. The Capitals traded former captain Bill Clement to Calgary in 1976. What did they receive?

    a. Jean Lemieux, Gerry Meehan, and a 1st round draft pick
    b. Two 2nd round draft picks
    c. A 1st and 2nd round draft pick
    d. Cash

16. In March 1997, Washington acquired Adam Oates, Rick Tocchet, and goaltender Bill Ranford in a blockbuster trade with the Boston Bruins.

    a. True
    b. False

17. The Capitals acquired which player from the Los Angeles Kings on February 10, 1995, and then traded him to the Toronto Maple Leafs the same day?

   a. Randy Burridge
   b. Warren Rychel
   c. Mike Eagles
   d. Igor Ulanov

18. Peter Zezel and Mike Lalor were acquired by Washington in a 1990 trade with the St. Louis Blues. Who headed to St. Louis?

   a. John Tucker
   b. Rob Whistle
   c. Geoff Courtnall
   d. Torrie Robertson

19. The Capitals traded their 1983 1st round draft pick to the Winnipeg Jets for Dave Christian. Who did Winnipeg pick with the 14th overall draft pick?

   a. Bobby Dollas
   b. Dale Hawerchuk
   c. Dave Ellett
   d. Randy Carlyle

20. Dennis Maruk was traded to Washington from the Toronto Maple Leafs in 1976.

   a. True
   b. False

QUIZ ANSWERS

1. C – Rod Langway

2. A – True

3. C – A 3rd round draft pick

4. B – Colorado Avalanche

5. D – Marcus Johansson

6. A – Goaltender Pheonix Copley

7. B – False

8. B – A 1st and 2nd round draft pick

9. D – Jeff Schultz

10. C – Buffalo Sabres

11. A – Brian MacLellan

12. A – True

13. D – Jaynen Rissling

14. D – Doug Mohns

15. A – Jean Lemieux, Gerry Meehan, and a 1st round draft pick

16. A – True

17. B – Warren Rychel

18. C – Geoff Courtnall

19. A – Bobby Dollas

20. B – False

DID YOU KNOW?

1. General manager David Poile made one of the worst trades in Capitals history when he sent center Dennis Maruk to the Minnesota North Stars in 1983 for a 2nd round draft pick. Poile used the 34th overall pick in 1984 to take Stephen Leach. Maruk had scored 182 goals for the Caps in 343 regular-season games. He had seasons of 50, 60, and 31 goals and also set a club record with 136 points in 1981-82. Maruk would stay with Minnesota until 1989. Leach would play parts of five seasons in Washington with his best campaign being 32 points.

2. Poile also made one of the best trades ever for the Caps when he picked up defenseman Rod Langway from the Montreal Canadiens. Poile made the deal in August 1982 just 10 days after being named the youngest GM in the NHL at the time. It was blockbuster move which saw Washington deal team captain Ryan Walter and defender Rick Green for forwards Craig Laughlin and Doug Jarvis as well as blueliners Rod Langway and Brian Engblom. Washington made the playoffs for the first time the next season as Langway would go on to captain the team for almost 11 seasons. He also won a pair of Norris Trophies with the Caps as the league's top defenseman.

3. Washington made another shrewd deal in October 1983 when they sent defender Brian Engblom and forward Ken

Houston to the Los Angeles Kings for rearguard Larry Murphy. After 453 games with Washington, Murphy had racked up 86 goals and 345 points, and he would end up in the Hockey Hall of Fame.

4. Another bad trade by Washington saw the team send prospect Filip Forsberg to the Nashville Predators in April 2013 for fellow forwards Michael Latta and Martin Erat. Latta would score just four goals and 17 points with the Caps, while Erat would rack up two goals and 25 points. Meanwhile, Forsberg, who was drafted 11th overall by Washington in 2012, had 145 goals and 305 points in 395 regular-season games with Nashville heading into 2019-20, with 23 goals and 44 points in 61 playoff outings.

5. The first four trades in Washington history came in 1974, the year the team entered the NHL. These trades all involved cash. General manager Milt Schmidt acquired Doug Mohns, Tommy Williams, Bill Lesuk, and Andre Peloffy all for money before the season faced off. Mohns would make history by being named the club's first captain.

6. It may be hard to believe, but the Capitals made another monumental blunder in January 2004 when they sent Jaromir Jagr packing to the New York Rangers for fellow forward Anson Carter. Jagr scored 201 points in 190 regular-season games with Washington, with 7 points in 6 postseason games. Carter played just 19 regular-season games with the Caps and posted 10 points. Jagr finished his career with 766 goals and 1,921 points in 1,733 regular-

season games, won numerous trophies, and will be inducted into the Hockey Hall of Fame as soon as he's eligible.

7. Let's give the Capitals credit where it's due, though. The club originally acquired Jaromir Jagr from the Pittsburgh Penguins in July 2001 and only gave up Kris Beech, Ross Lupaschuk, and Michal Sivek in return, as well as future considerations. The Caps also picked up Frantisek Kucera in the deal.

8. Former Capitals captain Dale Hunter was traded by the team near the end of the season in 1998-99. He went to the Colorado Avalanche along with a 3rd round draft pick in 2000. The Caps received a 2nd round draft pick in 1999 and used it to take Charlie Stephens 31st overall. Hunter, who was one of the most popular Washington players ever, played just 12 games with Colorado and retired at the end of the season, while Stephens never played a game with the Caps and ended up back in Colorado where he played a grand total of eight regular-season games.

9. Dave Hanson, who portrayed one of the famous Hanson Brothers on the classic hockey movie *Slapshot* was thought by many people to have been traded by Washington in a roundabout way in June 1975. The Capitals sent their 11th round draft pick in 1975 to the Detroit Red Wings for cash. Detroit then drafted Hanson with the 176th pick overall. However, on closer inspection, it turned out to be a different Dave Hanson. The *Slapshot* Hanson did eventually play with the Red Wings in 1978-79.

10. The first major trade by Washington came in their second year of existence in June 1975. The team traded their 1st round draft pick in 1975 to the Philadelphia Flyers and received Bill Clement, Don MacLean, and the Flyers' 1st round pick in return. Philadelphia used the pick, which turned out to be 1st overall, by taking Mel Bridgman. The Caps picked 18th overall and took Alex Forsyth. Clement would become Washington's captain, but it was a one-sided trade for Philadelphia.

CHAPTER 8:

DRAFT DAY

QUIZ TIME!

1. Between Washington's inception and 2019, how many players have the Capitals drafted?

   a. 397
   b. 441
   c. 482
   d. 501

2. As well as the NHL Entry Draft in 1974, the Capitals also acquired players via an NHL Expansion Draft the same year.

   a. True
   b. False

3. The first player the Capitals took in the 1974 NHL Entry Draft was also the 1st pick overall. Who was it?

   a. Mike Marson
   b. John Nazar
   c. Greg Joly
   d. John Paddock

4. How many players did the Capitals select in the 1974 NHL Entry Draft?

    a. 8
    b. 12
    c. 17
    d. 25

5. The fewest players drafted by the Capitals in a year was?

    a. 4
    b. 6
    c. 7
    d. 8

6. In which round did Washington make their first draft selection in 2017?

    a. 1st round
    b. 2nd round
    c. 4th round
    d. 5th round

7. As of 2019, the Capitals had eight seasons in which they didn't draft a player in the 1st round.

    a. True
    b. False

8. How many 1st round draft picks did the Capitals have in 1996?

    a. 0
    b. 1
    c. 2
    d. 3

9. Goaltender Ilya Samsonov played in just 26 regular-season games with Washington in 2019-20 after being drafted with what overall pick in the 1st round in 2015?

    a. 3rd
    b. 8th
    c. 12th
    d. 22nd

10. Defenseman John Carlson was drafted with the 27th overall pick in the 1st round in 2008. Which league was he drafted from?

    a. Western Hockey League
    b. Ontario Hockey League
    c. Quebec Major Junior Hockey League
    d. United States Hockey League

11. Which left winger was drafted in 2002 with the 13th overall pick in the 1st round?

    a. Zbynek Novak
    b. Matt Pettinger
    c. Alexander Semin
    d. Matthew Lahey

12. The Capitals had three 1st round draft picks in both 2002 and 2004.

    a. True
    b. False

13. How many goalies did the Caps draft between 1974 and 2019?

a. 21

b. 28

c. 42

d. 49

14. Washington has drafted how many players with German citizenship up until 2019?

    a. 0

    b. 3

    c. 7

    d. 12

15. What defenseman was drafted in the 1st round with the 17th pick in 1984 and would go on to score 227 goals and 677 points in 1,157 career NHL regular-season games?

    a. Dallas Eakins

    b. Kevin Hatcher

    c. Scott Stevens

    d. Darren Veitch

16. Washington's first two draft picks in 1989 were both goalies.

    a. True

    b. False

17. Washington drafted Bob Carpenter with the 3rd overall pick in 1981 and traded him to which team in 1986?

    a. Los Angeles Kings

    b. New York Rangers

    c. Pittsburgh Penguins

    d. Winnipeg Jets

18. Which Washington general manager drafted Jeff Greenlaw in the 1st round with the 19th overall pick in 1986?

    a. George McPhee
    b. Milt Schmidt
    c. Brian MacLellan
    d. Max McNab

19. Who was the first forward drafted by the Caps in the 1974 NHL Expansion Draft?

    a. Dave Kryskow
    b. Simon Nolet
    c. Mike Bloom
    d. Steve West

20. Byron Dafoe was the highest-drafted goalie by the Caps with the 35th overall pick in 1989.

    a. True
    b. False

QUIZ ANSWERS

1. B – 441

2. A – True

3. C – Greg Joly

4. D – 25

5. A – 4

6. C – 4th round

7. B – False

8. C – 2

9. D – 22nd

10. D – United States Hockey League

11. C – Alexander Semin

12. A – True

13. C – 42

14. C – 7

15. B – Kevin Hatcher

16. A – True

17. B – New York Rangers

18. D – Max McNab

19. A – Dave Kryskow

20. B – False

DID YOU KNOW?

1. In 1974, when the Capitals drafted for the very first time, they took a goaltender named Johnny Bower in the 18th round with the 231st overall pick. Unfortunately, this wasn't the Hall of Fame goalie Johnny Bower who won four Stanley Cups with the Toronto Maple Leafs while playing in the NHL between 1953-54 and 1969-70.

2. The Capitals did land a goalie from the Toronto Maple Leafs in 1974, however, when they selected Ron Low with their first pick in the Expansion Draft. Low would go on to play in 147 regular-season contests with Washington between 1974-75 and 1976-77 with a wins-losses-ties record of 30-94-9. He posted one shutout, which was the first in team history.

3. Washington had three 1st round draft picks in 2002 and 2004. They selected defenseman Steve Eminger with the 12th overall pick in 2002 and followed up by taking winger Alexander Semin with the very next pick and center Boyd Gordon with the 17th selection. In 2004, they chose winger Alexander Ovechkin 1st overall with defenders Jeff Schultz and Mike Green going 27th and 29th, respectively.

4. One of the worst drafts ever for the Caps was 1995 as they chose Brad Church with the 17th overall pick in the 1st round and took fellow winger Miika Elomo with the 23rd choice. Each player skated just two games in the NHL and

combined for a lone assist. The team drafted 10 players that year, and they combined for 167 NHL contests between them.

5. The biggest 1st round bust for the Capitals was Alexander Kharlamov in 1994. The Caps took the Russian center 15th overall, and he failed to play a game in the NHL. Defender Sasha Pokulok also failed to play a single NHL contest after being taken 14th overall in 2005. The same could be said of center Anton Gustafsson, who went 21st in 2008.

6. The most successful lowest-round player drafted by the Caps so far has been winger Richard Zednik. He was taken in the 10th round with the 249th overall pick in 1994. Zednik went on to play 745 regular-season NHL games with 200 goals and 379 points to his name.

7. The 2007 Draft was arguably the worst for the Capitals as just one of the 10 players selected went on to play in the NHL. Defenseman Karl Alzner was taken with the 5th overall pick in the 1st round and played 686 regular-season NHL contests. He totaled 20 goals and 130 points.

8. The highest-scoring player taken by Washington in the 1974 NHL Expansion Draft ended up being left winger Denis Dupere. He was taken with the 20th overall selection in the draft which also included fellow expansion team the Kansas City Scouts. Dupere played 229 regular-season NHL outings and registered 51 goals and 106 points. He scored 20 goals and 35 points in 53 games in his lone season with the Caps.

9. Washington also took several players in the Expansion Draft of 1974 who didn't pan out. Center Randy Wyrozub was taken from the Buffalo Sabres, center Steve West was taken from the Minnesota North Stars, and winger Ron Anderson was chosen from the Boston Bruins, and none of them played another NHL game. Center Bob Collyard from the St. Louis Blues suffered the same fate.

10. The highest-drafted goaltender in Caps history was Olaf Kolzig who was taken in the 1st round with the 19th overall pick in 1989. The team has drafted just three netminders in the opening round, as Ilya Samsonov was taken 22nd in 2015 and Semyon Varlamov went 23rd in 2006.

CHAPTER 9:

GOALTENDER TIDBITS

QUIZ TIME!

1. Who was the first Washington goalie to capture the Vezina Trophy in 1995-96?

    a. Ron Low

    b. Jim Carey

    c. Olaf Kolzig

    d. Braden Holtby

2. Netminder Michel Belhumeur's wins-losses-ties record in the Capitals' inaugural season was 0-24-3.

    a. True

    b. False

3. How many assists did Olaf Kolzig record while playing goalie with the Caps?

    a. 0

    b. 6

    c. 17

    d. 21

4. Which Capitals goalie served the most penalty minutes at 114 while playing with the team?

    a. Don Beaupre
    b. Olaf Kolzig
    c. Al Jensen
    d. Pete Peeters

5. How did Washington acquire goalie Jose Theodore?

    a. Was drafted by the Capitals
    b. Was picked up on waivers
    c. In a trade with Colorado
    d. Signed as a free agent

6. Braden Holtby and Olaf Kolzig share the team record for most games played in a season. How many did they play?

    a. 65
    b. 68
    c. 73
    d. 75

7. The fewest goals allowed in a regular season by Caps goalies was 194 in 1999-2000.

    a. True
    b. False

8. Which goalie holds the team record for most wins by a rookie, with 27?

    a. Wayne Stephenson
    b. Michal Neuvirth
    c. Pat Riggin
    d. Semyon Varlamov

9. The most wins in a season for a Washington goalie is?

    a. 35

    b. 42

    c. 48

    d. 50

10. Braden Holtby signed a five-year contract with the Caps in 2015. How much was the total worth?

    a. $20 million

    b. $25 million

    c. $30.5 million

    d. $34 million

11. Which Caps goaltender posted a 1.63 goals-against average and .936 save percentage in 13 appearances in 2008?

    a. Corey Hirsch

    b. Cristobal Huet

    c. Tomas Vokoun

    d. Sebastien Charpentier

12. Although Olaf Kolzig represented Germany internationally, he was born in South Africa.

    a. True

    b. False

13. Which former Caps goalie once scored a goal against the New York Islanders while playing for the Montreal Canadiens in 2001?

    a. Brent Johnson

    b. Bill Ranford

c. Rick Tabaracci

d. Jose Theodore

14. How many shutouts did Don Beaupre record in his 269 games with Washington?

    a. 0

    b. 7

    c. 12

    d. 19

15. The lowest career save percentage while playing for the Caps was .833, which was accompanied by the highest goals-against average of 6.90. Which netminder recorded these numbers?

    a. Gary Smith

    b. Rollie Boutin

    c. Jim Bedard

    d. John Adams

16. The Capitals used 48 different goalies in the net between 1974 and 2019.

    a. True

    b. False

17. How many goalies played just one career game for the Caps?

    a. 0

    b. 4

    c. 7

    d. 12

18. Which of these goalies did not play for Washington?

   a. Bruce Gamble
   b. Roger Crozier
   c. Mike Liut
   d. Bill Ranford

19. What season did Capitals goalie Olaf Kolzig win the Vezina Trophy?

   a. 1997-98
   b. 1999-2000
   c. 2001-02
   d. 2003-04

20. Goalie Jim Carey was traded to the Los Angeles Kings in 1996-97.

   a. True
   b. False

QUIZ ANSWERS

11. B – Jim Carey

12. A – True

13. C – 17

14. A – Don Beaupre

15. D – Signed as a free agent

1. C – 73

2. A – True

3. B – Michal Neuvirth

4. C – 48

5. C – $30.5 million

6. B – Cristobal Huet

7. A – True

8. D – Jose Theodore

9. C – 12

10. D – John Adams

11. A – True

12. B – 4

13. A – Bruce Gamble

14. B – 1999-2000

15. B – False

DID YOU KNOW?

1. Five goalies never won a game while tending goal for the Capitals. Michel Belhumeur played in 42 regular-season games and posted a wins-losses-ties record of 0-29-4. However, he went 9-36-7 in his NHL career in 65 games, as he went 9-7-3 with the Philadelphia Flyers in 1972-73. Belhumeur was acquired by Washington in the 1974 NHL Expansion Draft. The other four goalies who never won a game all appeared in fewer than nine contests with the team.

2. Three goalies have won Vezina Trophies while playing for the Caps. Jim Carey won the award in 1995-96, Olaf Kolzig took it home for 1999-2000, and Braden Holtby was named the winner in 2015-16. However, two other former Caps netminders won the Vezina with other clubs. Pete Peeters won it with the Boston Bruins in 1982-83, and Jose Theodore of the Montreal Canadiens was the recipient in 2001-02.

3. Olaf Kolzig has been the busiest netminder in Washington history so far. He played in 711 regular-season games. He also won, lost, and tied the most career games with the team at 301-293-63. In addition, Kolzig made the most saves in regular-season games in team history with 18,013 and faced the most shots against at 19,873.

4. Braden Holtby owns or shares 11 club records for regular-

season play. These include most games played in a season (73), most consecutive starts in a season (23), most wins in a season (48), most shutouts in a season (9), most shutouts in a career (35), most overtime defeats in a season (11), highest save percentage in a season with at least 20 games played (.925), highest career save percentage with at least 82 games played (.918), lowest goals-against average in a season with at least 20 games played (2.07), most saves in a season (1,887), and most shots against in a campaign (2,044).

5. The Capitals' record for most losses in one season was set in the team's inaugural campaign in 1974-75. Ron Low lost 36 games that year, but on the bright side, he was also credited with all eight of the team's victories too.

6. Clint Malarchuk played 96 times for Washington in 1988 and 1989 with a 40-38-11 record. He was then traded to Buffalo in March 1989. It was with the Sabres when Malarchuk nearly lost his life on the ice in a game. Just two weeks after being traded from Washington, the goalie suffered a severed jugular vein when an opposing player's skate blade sliced his neck.

7. In February 2020, Ilya Samsonov became just the third rookie in NHL history to win 11 consecutive regular-season games. The 22-year-old was also the fourth goalie in league annals to win 16 of his first 20 decisions and was 10-0 on the road at the time. Samsonov also set a new Caps record by winning 12 of his first 14 starts.

8. Jim Carey played just two seasons with Washington but is generally regarded as one of the club's top goalies. He was drafted 32nd overall by the Caps in 1992 and went 18-6-3 as a rookie in 1994-95, with a 2.13 goals-against average. He was a nominee for the Calder Trophy as the NHL's best rookie and also for the Vezina Trophy as the best goalie. However, he struggled in the playoffs. He bounced back the next season and won the Vezina while leading the league with nine shutouts. He struggled in the postseason again though and was soon sent to the Boston Bruins in a blockbuster trade.

9. The fewest goalies the Capitals have used in a season has been two. The most goalies to see action in one regular-season campaign has been five, which has happened on several occasions throughout the franchise's history. The last time five goalies saw action in the same season was 2003-04.

10. Pat Riggin was one of the Capitals' most underrated goalies as he played just over three seasons with the team. He posted the NHL's best goals-against average in 1983-84 at 2.67, to share the William Jennings Trophy with teammate Al Jensen. He was also named to the league's Second All-Star Team that season.

CHAPTER 10:

ODDS & ENDS

QUIZ TIME!

1. Ron Low posted the first shutout in Washington history on February 16, 1975. Which team did he beat 3-0?

    a. Kansas City Scouts

    b. Detroit Red Wings

    c. Vancouver Canucks

    d. Buffalo Sabres

2. Each Capitals player has his theme song played over the PA system when scoring a goal at home.

    a. True

    b. False

3. When Gary Green replaced Danny Belisle as the Caps head coach in 1979, he was the youngest coach in the NHL at the time. How old was he?

    a. 25

    b. 26

    c. 29

    d. 32

4. What year did the Capitals retire the jersey number of former captain Yvon Labre?

    a. 1978
    b. 1981
    c. 1996
    d. 2012

5. Dennis Maruk and which Caps teammate both scored three goals in the team's win over the Philadelphia Flyers in 1981?

    a. Tim Tookey
    b. Ryan Walter
    c. Bob Kelly
    d. Paul Mulvey

6. Which player led the Caps defensemen in scoring in 1980-81 with eight goals and 31 points?

    a. Darren Veitch
    b. Alan Hangsleben
    c. Rick Green
    d. Pat Ribble

7. Three Hall of Fame players were involved in the March 7, 1989, trade between the Caps and Minnesota North Stars. They were Dino Ciccarelli, Mike Gartner, and Larry Murphy.

    a. True
    b. False

8. What year did Washington host its first NHL All-Star Game?

a. 1979

b. 1982

c. 1987

d. 1993

9. The Caps beat which team 4-2 on the road on February 18, 1984, for their club record tenth straight regular-season win?

a. Calgary Flames

b. Dallas Stars

c. Carolina Hurricanes

d. St. Louis Blues

10. Which Washington head coach had a .500 points-percentage record with the team?

a. Jim Schoenfeld

b. Ron Wilson

c. Terry Murray

d. Bruce Cassidy

11. Which player has taken the most penalty shots in Caps history?

a. Mike Gartner

b. Alexander Ovechkin

c. Joe Sacco

d. Dainius Zubrus

12. Jack Egers scored the first Caps regular-season game-winning goal in 1974 in a 4-3 home win over the Chicago Blackhawks.

a. True

b. False

13. How many times did Washington make the playoffs between 1974 and 2019?

    a. 21
    b. 26
    c. 29
    d. 32

14. Yvon Labre scored Washington's first home goal on October 15, 1974, in a 1-1 tie with which team?

    a. Los Angeles Kings
    b. Toronto Maple Leafs
    c. St. Louis Blues
    d. Chicago Blackhawks

15. The longest game in Caps history ended in a 3-2 loss to which team at the 79:15 mark of overtime in 1996?

    a. Vancouver Canucks
    b. New York Islanders
    c. Pittsburgh Penguins
    d. Nashville Predators

16. Hall-of-Famer Mike Gartner's middle name was Alfred.

    a. True
    b. False

17. How many combined regular-season and playoff hat tricks have been scored by Caps players from 1974 to 2000?

a. 99

b. 121

c. 149

d. 233

18. Hall of Fame blueliner Rod Langway was born in which country?

    a. Canada

    b. America

    c. Sweden

    d. Taiwan

19. Capitals current captain Alexander Ovechkin is well known for wearing what color of skate laces?

    a. White

    b. Black

    c. Yellow

    d. Pink

20. The Capitals have hosted five NHL All-Star Games between 1974 and 2020.

    a. True

    b. False

QUIZ ANSWERS

1. A – Kansas City Scouts

2. A – True

3. B – 26

4. B – 1981

5. A – Tim Tookey

6. C – Rick Green

7. A – True

8. B – 1982

9. D – St. Louis Blues

10. D – Bruce Cassidy

11. B – Alexander Ovechkin

12. A – True

13. C – 29

14. A – Los Angeles Kings

15. C – Pittsburgh Penguins

16. A – True

17. C – 149

18. D – Taiwan

19. C – Yellow

20. B – False

DID YOU KNOW?

1. Mike Palmateer was acquired from the Toronto Maple Leafs in a trade in June 1980. He was nicknamed "The Popcorn Kid" due to his habit of eating the snack before every game. When playing for Washington in 1980-81, Palmateer set a new NHL record at the time for assists in a season by a goaltender with eight.

2. Winger Dino Ciccarelli is one of eight players who dressed for the Capitals and ended up in the Hockey Hall of Fame. He proved all the critics wrong as he was never drafted into the NHL but played 19 seasons in the league from 1980 to 1999. Ciccarelli was acquired by Washington in a 1989 trade with the Minnesota North Stars. He became the first Caps player to score seven points in a game and notched 209 points in 223 regular-season contests with Washington. Ciccarelli finished his career with 608 goals and 1,200 points in 1,232 outings.

3. On February 4, 2020, Alexander Ovechkin scored the 28th hat trick of his NHL career. This moved him into 8th place on the all-time list for three-goal games in the league. This meant Ovechkin had scored 14 of the team's last 18 hat tricks. In addition, between December 29, 2007, and February 7, 2010, Ovechkin scored all eight hat tricks that the team recorded. On an odd note, all but one of Ovechkin's three-goal games have been in regular-season action.

4. "The Easter Epic" refers to the second-longest game in Capitals history. It started on April 18, 1987, and finished at 1:58 a.m. on Easter Sunday the next morning. The home game concluded six hours and eighteen minutes after the opening faceoff. It ended when Pat LaFontaine scored at the 8:47 mark of the fourth overtime period to give the visiting New York Islanders Game 7 of the Patrick Division Semifinals. It was the first NHL game to go to four overtime periods since 1951.

5. The Capitals won the rights to an NHL franchise on June 9, 1972. They entered the league two years later in time for the 1974-75 campaign. The Kansas City Scouts also entered the league at the same time, and the two teams became the 17th and 18th NHL franchises at the time. Other cities which tried to earn an expansion franchise at the time were Dallas, Cincinnati, San Diego, Cleveland, Phoenix, and Indianapolis.

6. The Capitals have been awarded a combined 67 regular-season and playoff penalty shots since the team's NHL debut. The first one came in December 1974 when Tommy Williams was foiled against the Buffalo Sabres. The first successful attempt came from the stick of Steve Atkinson on February 1, 1975, on the club's second attempt in a game against the Vancouver Canucks. Alexander Ovechkin has taken the most penalty shots but has scored on just two of his 12 attempts.

7. Washington has had 18 different head coaches between 1974 and 2020, with Jim Anderson being the first. The only

coaches who didn't play in the NHL were Tom McVie, Gary Green, Bryan Murray, and Barry Trotz. The remainder of the coaches are Todd Reirden, Adam Oates, Dale Hunter, Bruce Boudreau, Glen Hanlon, Bruce Cassidy, Ron Wilson, Jim Schoenfeld, Terry Murray, Roger Crozier, Danny Belisle, Milt Schmidt, and Red Sullivan.

8. Most hockey fans know just how bad the Capitals' debut season in the NHL was, with eight wins and just 21 points. However, they may not realize their sophomore season wasn't much better. The squad went 25 straight games at one point in 1975-76 and surrendered 394 goals in the season. They finished the campaign with a record 11-59-10 for 32 points. In addition, general manager Milt Schmidt was fired midway through the season and replaced by Max McNab as GM and by Tom McVie as head coach.

9. Capitals fans, players, and coaches were heartbroken in both 1979-80 and 1980-81 as the team once again missed the playoffs. To make matters worse, though, they were eliminated from postseason contention on the very last day of the season. Washington finished two points behind the Edmonton Oilers for the final playoff spot in 1980 and a single point behind the Toronto Maple Leafs the next year.

10. When the Capitals won the Stanley Cup for the first time in 2017-18 with a five-game triumph over the expansion Vegas Golden Knights, it was cause for the locals to celebrate. The victory was the first major sports championship for a Washington, D.C., franchise since the

Washington Redskins captured the NFL's Super Bowl on January 26, 1992. Neither the city's NBA nor MLB teams had won a title in between. However, D.C. United of Major League Soccer (MLS) won the MLS Cup four times between 1996 and 2004.

CHAPTER 11:

CAPITALS ON THE BLUE LINE

QUIZ TIME!

1. How many defensemen have won the James Norris Trophy while playing with the Caps?

    a. 0

    b. 1

    c. 2

    d. 4

2. Scott Stevens was drafted by the Capitals but won a Norris Trophy with the New Jersey Devils.

    a. True

    b. False

3. Which Capitals blueliner scored 34 goals in a season with the team?

    a. Kevin Hatcher

    b. Darren Veitch

    c. John Carlson

    d. Robert Picard

4. How many Caps defenders were drafted 1st overall in the NHL?

    a. 0
    b. 1
    c. 2
    d. 3

5. Darren Veitch was drafted 5th overall in 1980. What league was he drafted from?

    a. Western Hockey League
    b. United States Hockey League
    c. Ontario Hockey League
    d. Quebec Major Junior Hockey League

6. Which rearguard was not drafted by Washington?

    a. Timo Blomqvist
    b. Eric Calder
    c. Bob Rouse
    d. Sergei Gonchar

7. Tyson Barrie once patrolled the blue line for the Capitals.

    a. True
    b. False

8. How was Rod Langway acquired by Washington?

    a. Signed as a free agent
    b. Drafted by the team
    c. Claimed on waivers
    d. In a trade with the Montreal Canadiens

9. Which defender was drafted in the 1st round by Washington with the 27th overall pick and would play just 21 NHL games?

   a. Joe Finley
   b. Keith Seabrook
   c. Mark Matier
   d. John Slaney

10. Which Caps defenseman scored 13 shorthanded goals with the team?

    a. Rod Langway
    b. Kevin Hatcher
    c. Larry Murphy
    d. Sylvain Cote

11. Scott Stevens was the most-penalized defender in Caps regular-season history. How many minutes did he serve?

    a. 2,003
    b. 1,628
    c. 1,220
    d. 1,189

12. Larry Murphy scored 120 power-play goals for the Caps in 453 regular-season games with the club.

    a. True
    b. False

13. Which Caps rearguard had a club-worst plus/minus record of -137 while playing for the team?

    a. Gord Smith
    b. Bill Mikkelson

c. Rick Green

d. Brendan Witt

14. Which defender drafted 55th overall by the Caps would play just one NHL contest in his career?

a. Blair MacKasey

b. Peter Scamurra

c. Don Wilson

d. Brent Tremblay

15. What number did Brad Schlegel wear with Washington in 1992-93?

a. 7

b. 14

c. 21

d. 28

16. Defenseman Paul Cavallini had two different stints with the Capitals.

a. True

b. False

17. How many points did Calle Johansson score from the blue line in 1992-93?

a. 21

b. 45

c. 49

d. 57

18. Which Capitals defenseman scored a hat trick against the New York Islanders in April 1993?

a. Shawn Anderson

b. Sylvain Cote

c. Jason Woolley

d. Al Iafrate

19. Which defenseman was drafted the lowest in team history with the 289th overall pick?

a. Johnny Oduya

b. Igor Shadilov

c. Bjorn Nord

d. Oscar Hedman

20. Defenseman Nolan Baumgartner was drafted in the 1st round with the 10th overall pick in 1994.

a. True

b. False

QUIZ ANSWERS

1. B – 1

2. B – False

3. A – Kevin Hatcher

4. C – 2

5. A – Western Hockey League

6. C – Bob Rouse

7. B – False

8. D – In a trade with the Montreal Canadiens

9. A – Joe Finley

10. B – Kevin Hatcher

11. B – 1,628

12. A – True

13. C – Rick Green

14. A – Blair MacKasey

15. D – 28

16. A – True

17. B – 45

18. D – Al Iafrate

19. C – Bjorn Nord

20. A – True

DID YOU KNOW?

1. Just one player has won the James Norris Trophy while playing with Washington. Hall-of-Famer Rod Langway won the award in 1982-83 and 1983-84. He netted three goals and 32 points in 1982-83 and had a plus/minus mark of -2. The next season he notched nine goals and 33 points with a +14 rating. The former Caps captain played 726 regular-season games in Washington with 25 goals, 202 points, and a +116 ranking.

2. Hall-of-Famer Scott Stevens was drafted in the 1st round by Washington with the 5th overall pick in 1982. He would go on to win three Stanley Cups and a Conn Smythe Trophy, and was a five-time All-Star. However, most of his accolades would come as a member of the New Jersey Devils. Stevens played the first eight seasons of his career with the Caps, then spent a year in St. Louis and another 14 campaigns in New Jersey. Washington lost him in the summer of 1990 when he signed as a free agent with the Blues.

3. When the Capitals entered the NHL in 1974-75, there was a ton of pressure on young defenseman Greg Joly who was drafted 1st overall a few months earlier. Joly struggled with the rest of the team as a 20-year-old rookie. He managed just one goal, which came on the power-play, and eight points in 44 games. In his second season, Joly

registered a much improved eight goals and 25 points with seven power-play markers. He also improved his plus/minus to -47. He was then traded to Detroit in 1976 and finished his nine-year career with 21 goals and 97 points and was a -165.

4. Another defenseman who was drafted 1st overall by Washington was Rick Green in 1976. Green played six seasons with the team with 31 goals and 158 points to his name in 377 regular-season outings. However, his plus/minus mark of -137 still stands as the worst number in club history. Green was a part of the blockbuster trade with the Montreal Canadiens in 1982 which saw Rod Langway come to Washington. Green then won a Stanley Cup with Montreal in 1985-86.

5. Kevin Hatcher set the franchise records for goals by a defenseman in one season in 1992-93. He tallied 34 goals that year and added 45 assists for 79 points. Hatcher was drafted in the 1st round by the Caps with the 17th overall pick in 1984. He tallied 149 goals and 277 assists for Washington in 685 career games. Hatcher finished his career with 227 goals and 677 points in 1,157 career regular-season contests. The Caps traded him to the Dallas Stars in 1994.

6. John Carlson was an important piece of the puzzle in 2017-18 when the Capitals won the Stanley Cup for the first time in franchise history. Carlson chipped in with five goals and 20 points to lead the team's blueliners in its five-

game win over the Vegas Golden Knights. He notched four power-play goals in the series and averaged 25:38 minutes of ice time per game.

7. Defenseman Pierre Bouchard spent the last four seasons of his 12-year career in Washington after being acquired from the Montreal Canadiens in 1978-79. Bouchard was the son of Hall-of-Famer Butch Bouchard who won four Stanley Cups patrolling the blue line with Montreal. Pierre went one better, though, as he won five cups with the Habs between 1970 and 1978.

8. The first Washington Capital to technically have his name engraved on the Stanley Cup was defender Gord Lane. He played with the Caps from 1975-76 to 1979-80 when he was traded midway through the season to the New York Islanders. Lane was then fortunate enough to win four Stanley Cups with the Islanders with the first one coming just months after joining the team.

9. Robert Picard was drafted 3rd overall by Washington in 1977 and then signed a deal with the club. However, he then found out he could earn a bigger paycheck if he joined the World Hockey Association (WHA). This led the native of Montreal to sign a contract with the Quebec Nordiques of the WHA. The WHA wouldn't allow Picard to play in the league though since they knew they would face a lawsuit from the Capitals and the WHA. Picard would play the first 230 games of his career in Washington. He would eventually play 289 games with Quebec between 1985 and 1990.

10. Veteran defenseman Brooks Orpik joined the Caps in 2014 and helped the team win the Stanley Cup four years later. He was then traded just days after the championship parade to the Colorado Avalanche with backup goalie Philipp Grubauer. The trade enabled Washington to clear up $5.5 million of salary, which helped them re-sign top blueliner John Carlson. Orpik was then bought out by Colorado.

CHAPTER 12:

CENTERS OF ATTENTION

QUIZ TIME!

1. Which Capitals center would later become head coach of the team?

    a. Dennis Maruk

    b. Sergei Fedorov

    c. Adam Oates

    d. Eric Fehr

2. Center Mikhail Grabovski wore number 84 in 2014.

    a. True

    b. False

3. Which center was not drafted by the Capitals?

    a. Mathieu Perreault

    b. Luke Lynes

    c. Brian Sutherby

    d. Steve Sullivan

4. Which center was drafted by the Caps in the 1st round with the 25th overall pick in 2019?

a. Aliaksei Protas

b. Connor McMichael

c. Garrett Pilon

d. Brian Pinho

5. Cody Eakin was drafted in the 3rd round with the 85th overall pick in 2009. What league was he drafted from?

a. Western Hockey League

b. United States Hockey League

c. Ontario Hockey League

d. Quebec Major Junior Hockey League

6. Which center did the Caps draft with the 213th overall pick in 1978. He would score 86 points in 237 career NHL games.

a. Wes Jarvis

b. Glen Currie

c. Tim Tookey

d. Chris Valentine

7. Center Bob Carpenter scored 32 goals and 67 points for the Caps as an 18-year-old rookie.

a. True

b. False

8. How was center Dale Hunter acquired by Washington?

a. Signed as a free agent

b. Drafted by the team

c. Claimed on waivers

d. In a trade with the Quebec Nordiques

9. How many Capitals centers have had their jersey numbers retired by the team?

    a. 0

    b. 1

    c. 2

    d. 3

10. Which center scored the franchise's first hat trick?

    a. Walt McKechnie

    b. Risto Jalo

    c. Ron Lalonde

    d. Jack Patterson

11. Which center was drafted 36th overall in 1988 but was traded before ever playing a game with Washington?

    a. Tim Taylor

    b. Reggie Savage

    c. Todd Hlushko

    d. Brian Sakic

12. Filip Forsberg was drafted by the Caps with the 11th overall selection in 2012.

    a. True

    b. False

13. How many Caps centers scored hat tricks in the team's 10-4 win over the Philadelphia Flyers in November 1981?

    a. 0

    b. 1

    c. 2

    d. 3

14. How many points did pivot Tim Tookey register with the team in just 29 games in 1980-81?

    a. 19
    b. 23
    c. 29
    d. 32

15. Which Caps player was the first team center to score on an NHL penalty shot for the club?

    a. Nelson Pyatt
    b. Dennis Maruk
    c. Bob Carpenter
    d. Ron Poole

16. Former Caps center Guy Charron played 734 regular-season games without playing in one playoff game, which is an NHL record.

    a. True
    b. False

17. Which Washington center won the Selke Award as the NHL's best defensive forward for 1983-84?

    a. Bengt Gustafsson
    b. Dave Christian
    c. Glen Currie
    d. Doug Jarvis

18. How many career shorthanded goals did center Mike Ridley score for the Capitals?

a. 0

b. 5

c. 12

d. 17

19. Dale Hunter scored how many career game-winning goals for Washington?

    a. 14

    b. 21

    c. 29

    d. 42

20. In January 1984, Bengt Gustafsson was the first Caps player to score four goals in a game.

    a. True

    b. False

QUIZ ANSWERS

1. C – Adam Oates

2. A – True

3. D – Steve Sullivan

4. B – Connor McMichael

5. A – Western Hockey League

6. A – Wes Jarvis

7. A – True

8. D – In a trade with the Quebec Nordiques

9. B – 1

10. C – Ron Lalonde

11. A – Tim Taylor

12. A – True

13. C – 2

14. B – 23

15. A – Nelson Pyatt

16. A – True

17. D – Doug Jarvis

18. D – 17

19. C – 29

20. B – False

DID YOU KNOW?

1. The Capitals definitely strengthened their squad with the acquisition of center Dale Hunter in 1987. He was acquired in a trade with the Quebec Nordiques and would play 12 years with the team and later became the Caps' head coach. Hunter notched 181 goals and 556 points with the Capitals and displayed great leadership qualities. He never backed down from anyone and would serve a club record 2,003 minutes in penalties.

2. One of the steadiest and most consistent centers in Washington was Dave Christian, who was originally drafted 40th overall by the Winnipeg Jets in 1979. Washington traded their 1st round draft choice for Christian in 1983. He would play six full seasons and part of a seventh with the team and missed just six games over that stretch. Christian racked up 193 goals and 417 points with Washington in 504 games, with 36 points in 49 playoff games.

3. Center Nelson Pyatt was the first Capitals player to score 25 goals in a season. He achieved the feat in 1975-76, which was the team's second year of existence. Pyatt would play just 93 games with the club but was quite successful as he registered 32 goals and 59 points. He was originally acquired by Washington from

112

Detroit in a February 1975 trade which saw the Caps give up a 3rd round draft choice. Pyatt is also the father of former NHL player Taylor Pyatt.

4. A Capitals center who got the job done without much fanfare was Mike Ridley. He broke into the NHL in 1985-86 as a free agent and scored 22 goals and 65 points with the New York Rangers. The Caps traded Bob Carpenter and a 2nd round draft pick for Ridley in January 1987 and also picked up Bob Crawford and Kelly Miller in the deal. Ridley would score 218 goals and 547 points in 588 games with the Caps, with 60 more points in 76 postseason outings. He was also a great penalty killer who scored 17 shorthanded goals.

5. When center Joe Juneau scored in overtime against the Buffalo Sabres in June 1998, it put the Capitals in the Stanley Cup Final for the very first time. Juneau's game-winner came in Game 6 of the series against Buffalo. However, the Capitals would be swept in four straight games by the defending Stanley Cup champs the Detroit Red Wings in the Final. Juneau was acquired by Washington in a 1993-94 trade with the Boston Bruins for star defenseman Al Iafrate.

6. Jeff Halpern grew up in nearby Potomac, Maryland, with his family being Capitals fans. He also played in the local area as a youngster for the Little Caps hockey organization. Halpern played Ivy League hockey for Princeton and led his league in goals as both a junior

and senior. He was never drafted into the NHL but signed with the Capitals as a free agent and made the team in 1999. He was named captain in 2005-06 and scored 91 goals and 230 points for the franchise in two separate stints.

7. Center Brooks Laich had some big shoes to fill when he came over in a trade from the Ottawa Senators for fan favorite Peter Bondra. It didn't take long for Caps fans to appreciate the work ethic of the 20-year-old Laich though, and he also became a favorite. He wasn't a big scorer but still managed to notch 133 goals and 324 points in 742 contests with the Capitals, with 32 points in 65 playoff games. He chipped in with 42 power-play goals in Washington, with 10 shorthanded tallies and 24 game-winners.

8. When center Adam Oates arrived in Washington the Hall-of-Famer was nearing the end of his storied career. He arrived via a trade with the Boston Bruins as one of the best playmakers in NHL history. Oates had made a name for himself by centering scoring sensation Brett Hull while playing with the St. Louis Blues and managed to lead the league in assists twice while playing with the Caps. He captained the team in 1999-2000 and 2000-01 and coached the club from 2012 to 2014. Oates scored 73 goals and 363 points in 387 regular-season games with Washington.

9. Guy Charron was a rags-to-riches story, as he broke into the NHL as an undrafted 21-year-old with the

Montreal Canadiens in 1969-70. When the Capitals joined the league as an expansion team in 1974-75, the Kansas City Scouts joined too and that's where Charron ended up in December 1974. The Caps signed him as a free agent in 1976, and Charron was an instant hit. He didn't miss a game in his first three seasons and posted campaigns of 36, 38, and 28 goals. Charron was a late bloomer and was the Caps' captain in 1978-79. He posted 118 goals and 274 points in 320 regular-season outings as a Capital.

10. Michal Pivonka was an important player for the Capitals and played his entire 13-year NHL career with the club. He defected to North America from the former nation of Czechoslovakia and wound up with Washington in 1986, two years after the team drafted him. Pivonka played 825 regular-season games and registered 181 goals and 599 points. When he retired in 1999, he was the team's all-time leader in assists. He also added 55 points in 95 postseason contests.

CHAPTER 13:

THE WINGERS TAKE FLIGHT

QUIZ TIME!

1. Which of these former Caps wingers is in the Hockey Hall of Fame?

    a. Peter Bondra

    b. Mike Gartner

    c. Alexander Semin

    d. Keith Jones

2. Russian winger Dmitri Khristich also played center ice during his career.

    a. True

    b. False

3. Which right winger was drafted 93rd overall by the Caps in 2018?

    a. Brett Leason

    b. Kody Clark

    c. Riley Sutter

    d. Damien Riat

4. Which winger was not drafted by Washington?

   a. Paul Henderson
   b. Kris King
   c. Trevor Halverson
   d. Tim Kennedy

5. Which Caps winger holds the club record with 32 shorthanded goals?

   a. Tim Bergland
   b. Mike Gartner
   c. John Druce
   d. Peter Bondra

6. Which winger did the Caps draft with the 71st overall pick in 1978? He would score 140 points in 459 career NHL games.

   a. Eddy Godin
   b. Steve Barger
   c. Doug Patey
   d. Lou Franceschetti

7. Winger Rick Vaive played two seasons with the Capitals.

   a. True
   b. False

8. Which winger became the first Caps player to score four goals in a game?

   a. John Paddock
   b. Jim Thomson
   c. Stan Gilbertson
   d. Martin Gendron

9. How many stints did winger Richard Zednik have with Washington?

    a. 1
    b. 2
    c. 3
    d. 4

10. How many career regular-season games did winger Trevor Linden play with the Capitals?

    a. 0
    b. 12
    c. 28
    d. 79

11. How was winger Tom Wilson acquired by Washington?

    a. Via NHL Entry Draft
    b. Signed as a free agent
    c. Via trade with the Montreal Canadiens
    d. Claimed on waivers

12. Former Caps winger Joel Ward would enjoy an 11-year NHL career even though he was undrafted.

    a. True
    b. False

13. Which Washington winger is the club's all-time leading scorer?

    a. Mike Gartner
    b. Peter Bondra
    c. Alexander Ovechkin
    d. Alexander Semin

14. Who was the lowest-drafted winger in Caps history as the 284th pick in 2001?

    a. Mark Olafson
    b. Viktor Hubl
    c. Patric Blomdahl
    d. Bill Kovacs

15. Which Caps winger wore number 50 in 2007-08?

    a. Joe Motzko
    b. Brian Stagg
    c. Joni Lindlof
    d. Andrew Glass

16. Winger Tim Kennedy was drafted in the 1st round in 2005.

    a. True
    b. False

17. How many career NHL games did the Caps' 2002 draft pick Marian Havel play?

    a. 0
    b. 21
    c. 82
    d. 633

18. What year was Caps winger Alexander Ovechkin born?

    a. 1984
    b. 1985
    c. 1988
    d. 1989

19. Which team did Washington trade winger Craig Laughlin to in February 1988?

    a. Los Angeles Kings
    b. Toronto Maple Leafs
    c. Montreal Canadiens
    d. Edmonton Oilers

20. Winger Trent Klatt was drafted 82nd overall by Washington in 1989 but was traded before playing a game with the club.

    a. True
    b. False

QUIZ ANSWERS

1. B – Mike Gartner

2. A – True

3. C – Riley Sutter

4. A – Paul Henderson

5. D – Peter Bondra

6. D – Lou Franceschetti

7. B – False

8. C – Stan Gilbertson

9. B – 2

10. C – 28

11. A – Via NHL Entry Draft

12. A – True

13. C – Alexander Ovechkin

14. B – Viktor Hubl

15. A – Joe Motzko

16. B – False

17. A – 0

18. B – 1985

19. A – Los Angeles Kings

20. A – True

DID YOU KNOW?

1. Riley Sutter, who was drafted by Washington in the 3rd round with the 93rd overall pick in 2018, is a member of the famous Sutter family. Riley's father Ron Sutter enjoyed a 13-year NHL career, and five of his uncles also played in the league. These were Rich, Duane, Darryl, Brian, and Brent Sutter. In addition, three of Riley's cousins, Brody, Brett, and Brandon, have also played in the NHL.

2. Most hockey fans know that winger Alexander Ovechkin is the Capitals' all-time leading scorer and current captain. In fact, he's likely to be known as one of the greatest hockey players in history. However, you may not know that Ovechkin's superb athletic genes come from his parents. Alexander's mother Tatyana Ovechkina won two Olympic gold medals in basketball, and his father Mikhail played soccer.

3. Former Washington left winger Denis Dupere was the first NHLer to play with the Capitals, Kansas City Scouts, and Colorado Rockies franchises. Washington and Kansas City both entered the league in 1974-75, and Kansas then relocated to Colorado in 1976-77. Dupere was originally claimed by the Caps in the 1974 NHL Expansion Draft from the Toronto Maple Leafs. Washington traded him to the St. Louis Blues in February 1975, and the Blues swapped Dupere to Kansas City four months later.

4. One of the most successful wingers in Capitals history was Peter Bondra, who played with the team from 1990 to 2004. Bondra would score 472 goals and 353 assists in 961 regular-season games for the club for 825 points and contributed 30 goals and 56 points in 73 playoff games. He holds the club record for shorthanded goals at 32. Bondra twice led the NHL in goals scored in a season and retired in 2007 with 503 goals and 892 points in 1,081 regular-season contests.

5. When right winger Archie Henderson showed up for work with the Capitals in December of 1980, he made franchise history in a minor way. Henderson became the first Caps player other than a goaltender to wear a jersey number that was higher than 29. Since Henderson was the biggest player in team history at the time, at 6 feet 6 inches tall, the only sweater that would fit him was a goalie jersey. Therefore, he was given number 31 to wear.

6. The 1974-75 NHL season was rather forgettable for Washington as it was the franchise's first in the league, and they set records for futility. There was a bright light for winger Stan Gilbertson, though, as he became the first Caps player to notch four goals in a game. His feat came on the final day of the season when the Caps doubled the Pittsburgh Penguins 8-4. Gilbertson scored 11 goals and 18 points for Washington in 25 games that campaign and would be traded to Pittsburgh midway through the next season.

7. Winger Tom Rowe scored on his very first shift in his NHL debut in 1976-77 when the Capitals visited the Bruins at Boston Garden. The youngster beat Hall of Fame netminder Gerry Cheevers to start his big-league career with a bang, but it would be the only goal he scored that year. Rowe added a pair of assists in the campaign and played just 12 games. He became a regular the next season and scored 31 times for the team in 1978-79 to become the first American-born player to notch 30 goals in the league.

8. The Capitals didn't play their first NHL playoff game until April 6, 1983, which was nine seasons after entering the league. Right winger Bobby Gould made franchise history by becoming the first Washington player to score a goal in the postseason. The Caps lost the game, though, as they were downed 5-2 by the powerful New York Islanders. Gould played 600 regular-season games for Washington, with 134 goals and 276 points, plus 12 goals and 24 points in 50 playoff outings.

9. The first five-goal game in the NHL by a Caps player was achieved by winger Bengt Gustafsson on January 8, 1984. Each of Gustafsson's five shots on the net in the game beat the goaltender in a 7-1 away victory over the Philadelphia Flyers. Gustafsson played his entire nine-year career with Washington from 1979 to 1989. He tallied 195 goals and 554 points in 629 regular-season games, with 9 goals and 28 points in 32 playoff matches. He had five seasons with over 20 goals and another campaign with 32.

10. After breaking into the NHL in 1961-62, winger Tommy Williams was already a 34-year-old veteran when he was traded to Washington for cash by the Boston Bruins in 1974. Williams played his final two seasons with the Caps and led the team in scoring in their inaugural season with 22 goals and 58 points. Williams took the Capitals' first-ever penalty shot when he failed to score in Buffalo against the Sabres in a 9-2 loss in December 1974. It was the second and last penalty shot in his career as he failed to score against Toronto 11 years earlier.

CHAPTER 14:

THE HEATED RIVALRIES

QUIZ TIME!

1. The Capitals' first-ever playoff game in 1983 resulted in a 5-2 loss to which team?

    a. New York Rangers

    b. New York Islanders

    c. Pittsburgh Penguins

    d. Hartford Whalers

2. The Capitals have met the Toronto Maple Leafs five times in the playoffs.

    a. True

    b. False

3. Washington swept which team in three straight games in 1984 to win their first postseason series?

    a. Quebec Nordiques

    b. Edmonton Oilers

    c. Buffalo Sabres

    d. Philadelphia Flyers

4. The longest Game 7 in playoff history was between Washington and which rival?

    a. New York Rangers
    b. Pittsburgh Penguins
    c. Philadelphia Flyers
    d. New York Islanders

5. Who scored the overtime winner in 1988 when the Caps beat the Philadelphia Flyers in Game 7 of their playoff series?

    a. Dale Hunter
    b. Kevin Hatcher
    c. Kelly Miller
    d. Bill Houlder

6. Washington advanced to the Eastern Conference Final for the first time in 1990 when which player scored in overtime on the road to eliminate the New York Rangers?

    a. Mike Ridley
    b. Michal Pivonka
    c. John Druce
    d. Neil Sheehy

7. Mikhail Grabovski scored three goals against the Chicago Blackhawks in his very first game for Washington on opening night 2013-14.

    a. True
    b. False

8. The Capitals and Pittsburgh Penguins have played in the

Metropolitan Division since 2013. Between 2015-16 and 2018-19 the teams met how many times, including playoff games?

   a. 26

   b. 30

   c. 36

   d. 40

9. Which team did the Caps beat 7-0 in the regular-season in 2013 in a game which featured a famous line brawl?

   a. Carolina Hurricanes

   b. Tampa Bay Lightning

   c. Philadelphia Flyers

   d. Columbus Blue Jackets

10. Which Washington rival played with them in the Patrick Division from 1981 to 1993?

   a. Los Angeles Kings

   b. Edmonton Oilers

   c. Toronto Maple Leafs

   d. Pittsburgh Penguins

11. Who scored the winning goal for the Pittsburgh Penguins at 19:15 of the fourth overtime to eliminate the Caps in their longest-ever playoff game in April 1996?

   a. Mario Lemieux

   b. Jaromir Jagr

   c. Petr Nedved

   d. Brad Lauer

12. The Capitals have played the Tampa Bay Lightning in seven playoff series.

    a. True
    b. False

13. Center Joe Juneau scored the overtime winner against which team in Game 6 of their playoff series to propel Washington to the 1997-98 Stanley Cup Final?

    a. Buffalo Sabres
    b. Detroit Red Wings
    c. Toronto Maple Leafs
    d. Boston Bruins

14. Which Eastern rival beat Washington in seven games in the 1st round of the 2018-19 playoffs?

    a. Carolina Hurricanes
    b. Columbus Blue Jackets
    c. Tampa Bay Lightning
    d. Toronto Maple Leafs

15. How many games did it take Washington to eliminate the Tampa Bay Lightning in the 2017-18 playoffs?

    a. 4
    b. 5
    c. 6
    d. 7

16. When Alexander scored three goals against Pittsburgh in May 2009, it was the first Caps playoff hat trick in over 16 years.

a. True

b. False

17. Which rivals beat the Capitals in seven games in the 2009-10 Eastern Conference quarterfinals?

    a. New York Rangers

    b. New York Islanders

    c. New Jersey Devils

    d. Montreal Canadiens

18. The Capitals lost at home to which rival in Game 7 of the 1987-88 Division Finals?

    a. New Jersey Devils

    b. Pittsburgh Penguins

    c. Philadelphia Flyers

    d. New York Rangers

19. Which of these teams has Washington never met in the playoffs?

    a. Los Angeles Kings

    b. Toronto Maple Leafs

    c. Montreal Canadiens

    d. Vegas Golden Knights

20. The Caps defeated their rivals the Pittsburgh Penguins in the Stanley Cup Final in 2017-18.

    a. True

    b. False

QUIZ ANSWERS

1. B – New York Islanders

2. B – False

3. D – Philadelphia Flyers

4. D – New York Islanders

5. A – Dale Hunter

6. C – John Druce

7. A – True

8. C – 36

9. C – Philadelphia Flyers

10. D – Pittsburgh Penguins

11. C – Petr Nedved

12. B – False

13. A – Buffalo Sabres

14. A – Carolina Hurricanes

15. D – 7

16. A – True

17. D – Montreal Canadiens

18. A – New Jersey Devils

19. A – Los Angeles Kings

20. B – False

DID YOU KNOW?

1. The Capitals and Pittsburgh Penguins rivalry has intensified since Sidney Crosby entered the league for Pittsburgh and Alexander Ovechkin joined the Caps. One of their greatest matchups came in Game 2 of the 2nd round of the 2008-09 playoffs. This was the first year the two stars met in the postseason. Both Crosby and Ovechkin netted hat tricks as the Caps won the game 4-3 to take a 2-0 lead in the series at home. They ended up losing the series in seven games though.

2. The bitter rivalry between Washington and Pittsburgh was on display in 2011-12 when there was at least one fight in all four of their regular-season meetings. In addition, the two Metropolitan Division rivals failed to shake hands on the ice following the 2011 Winter Classic Game in which Sidney Crosby was injured. Overall, the teams have met 11 times in playoffs, including three straight meetings between 2016 and 2018. The Penguins have won 9 of the 11 series, and this rivalry is considered one of the biggest and best in the NHL.

3. On April 16, 1988, the Caps won their first best-of-seven playoff series by downing the Philadelphia Flyers in the 1st round. It was a series of comebacks as the Capitals trailed 3-1 in games and were then down 3-0 in the deciding contest. Dale Hunter was the hero as he scored at 5:57 of overtime to give Washington a dramatic 5-4 victory.

4. Geographically, the Philadelphia Flyers are the Capitals' biggest rivals, but they're also rivals on the ice. The teams have faced each other five times in the postseason, with Washington taking three of the series. The games are generally nasty in nature and have been that way since both clubs joined the Metropolitan Division in 2013.

5. The Capitals and New York Rangers became archrivals when they met each other five times in the playoffs over a stretch of seven seasons, with the Rangers taking three of the series. This included three consecutive matchups between 2011 and 2013. To make the rivalry more dramatic, four of the five series went the full seven games. Overall, the Metropolitan Division clubs have played nine playoff series, with the Rangers triumphing in five of them.

6. The Capitals and New York Islanders have battled each other in a total of seven playoff series, with the Islanders having their way in five of them. The teams met five straight times in the postseason from 1983 to 1987 easily getting under each other's skin. To add to the tension between the franchises' fans, former head coach Barry Trotz left the Capitals after winning the Stanley Cup in 2017-18 and joined the hated Islanders.

7. Former captain Dale Hunter didn't care who he played against as he displayed the same grit and determination against all rivals. He served 3,565 penalty minutes in his career and still found the time to score 323 goals and 1,020

points in 1,407 career regular-season games. Hunter is so far the only NHL player ever to post more than 1,000 points and serve over 3,000 minutes in penalties.

8. One of the most notorious Dale Hunter incidents came in a game with heated rivals the New York Islanders. The teams were playing in the 1992-93 Patrick Division Semifinals when Hunter hit Islanders center Pierre Turgeon with a vicious crosscheck from behind late in Game 6. Turgeon, who scored 58 goals that season, had just scored moments before Hunter injured him to give his team a 5-1 lead to eliminate the Caps. Hunter received a 21-game suspension for the cheap shot, which was the longest ban in NHL history at the time.

9. On April 28, 2009, Sergei Fedorov scored in the third period to give Washington a 2-1 victory at home over the New York Rangers in Game 7 of the Eastern Conference quarterfinals. It was the Caps' first playoff series triumph in 11 years and their first win in a Game 7 in over 21 seasons.

10. Washington has one of the worst records in NHL history when it comes to performances in Game 7s of playoff series. As of 2018-19, the Caps were 5-12 when going to the final and deciding game in a seven-game set. They were a woeful 2-10 at home in those contests and were 2-4 in overtime games.

CHAPTER 15:

THE AWARDS SECTION

QUIZ TIME!

1. Who was the first Caps player to win a major NHL award?

    a. Peter Bondra

    b. Mike Gartner

    c. Rod Langway

    d. Dale Hunter

2. Kevin Hatcher was the first Washington player to win the James Norris Trophy as the NHL's top defender.

    a. True

    b. False

3. Who was the first Caps coach to win the Jack Adams Award as NHL coach of the year?

    a. Terry Murray

    b. Bryan Murray

    c. Barry Trotz

    d. Adam Oates

4. Which Washington player was the first to take home the Frank Selke Trophy as the league's best defensive forward?

   a. Peter Bondra

   b. Doug Jarvis

   c. Jan Bulis

   d. Mike Eagles

5. Who was the second Caps goaltender to win the Vezina Trophy as the NHL's best?

   a. Olaf Kolzig

   b. Jim Carey

   c. Braden Holtby

   d. Roger Crozier

6. Which year did the Capitals win the NHL Draft Lottery to move from 3rd to 1st place in selection order?

   a. 1998

   b. 2000

   c. 2004

   d. 2007

7. Washington captured the Norris, Jack Adams, and Selke Trophies in 1983-84.

   a. True

   b. False

8. Which player became the first Capital to win the Calder Trophy as NHL rookie of the year?

   a. Greg Joly

   b. Bobby Carpenter

c. Jim Carey

d. Alexander Ovechkin

9. Which Washington player led the NHL in goals twice before the Rocket Richard Trophy was introduced for the league's top marksman?

a. Bobby Carpenter

b. Peter Bondra

c. Dino Ciccarelli

d. Mike Gartner

10. Who was the second Capitals coach to win the Jack Adams Award?

a. Bruce Boudreau

b. Ron Wilson

c. Jim Schoenfeld

d. Todd Reirden

11. How many Rocket Richard Trophies had Alexander Ovechkin won or shared up until 2020-21?

a. 3

b. 5

c. 8

d. 9

12. Washington Broadcaster Ron Weber won the Foster Hewitt Memorial Award for outstanding contributions to his profession and the sport of hockey in 2010.

a. True

b. False

13. The Art Ross Trophy for leading the NHL in points for a season has been won by how many Washington players?

    a. 0
    b. 1
    c. 2
    d. 3

14. Who was the first Capital to play in the NHL All-Star Game?

    a. Bill Clement
    b. Guy Charron
    c. Bob Sirois
    d. Denis Dupere

15. The number of Washington players named to the NHL's All-Rookie Teams as of 2019 is?

    a. 0
    b. 1
    c. 5
    d. 7

16. Olaf Kolzig won the King Clancy Memorial Trophy in 2005-06 for humanitarian contribution and leadership.

    a. True
    b. False

17. How many different Caps players have been named to the NHL's First or Second Team All-Star squads between 1974 and 2019?

    a. 4
    b. 9

c. 12

d. 14

18. The Bill Masterton Trophy for perseverance, sportsmanship, and dedication to hockey was won by which Caps player in 2010?

   a. Mike Knuble

   b. Jason Chimera

   c. Jose Theodore

   d. Tom Poti

19. How many President's Trophies have the Caps won for earning the most points in the regular season?

   a. 0

   b. 1

   c. 3

   d. 5

20. The Caps' Rod Langway was the first American to win the Norris Trophy even though he was born in Taiwan.

   a. True

   b. False

QUIZ ANSWERS

1. C – Rod Langway

2. B – False

3. B – Bryan Murray

4. B – Doug Jarvis

5. A – Olaf Kolzig

6. C – 2004

7. A – True

8. D – Alexander Ovechkin

9. B – Peter Bondra

10. A – Bruce Boudreau

11. D – 9

12. A – True

13. B – 1

14. D – Denis Dupere

15. D – 7

16. A – True

17. C – 12

18. C – Jose Theodore

19. C – 3

20. A – True

DID YOU KNOW?

1. The 2007-08 campaign was a special one for Alexander Ovechkin as he became the first player in the history of the NHL to win the Hart, Art Ross, Lester B. Pearson, and Rocket Richard Trophies all in the same season. As of 2019, Ovechkin had won a Calder Trophy, an Art Ross Trophy, a Conn Smythe Trophy, three Hart Trophies, three Ted Lindsay Awards, and eight Rocket Richard Trophies.

2. Rod Langway was the first Caps player to take home a major award when he snagged the James Norris Trophy as the league's top blueliner. He then won it again the very next season in 1983-84. Also, in 1983-84, Bryan Murray was handed the Jack Adams Award as top head coach in the NHL, and center Doug Jarvis captured the Frank Selke Trophy for being voted the best defensive forward.

3. Being named to the NHL's First or Second All-Star Team is quite an honor as it means you're one of the top players in the league at your position. Caps players named to a First All-Star Team are: goaltenders Jim Carey, Olaf Kolzig, and Braden Holtby; defensemen Scott Stevens, Mike Green (twice), Rod Langway (twice), and left winger Alexander Ovechkin (seven). Ovechkin was also named once as a right winger. Those named to a Second Team are: goaltenders Pat Riggin and Braden Holtby; defensemen Al Iafrate, John Carlson, Rod Langway, Larry Murphy, and Sergei Gonchar (twice).

4. The All-Rookie Team is similar to an all-star squad for the league's first-year players. Washington youngsters who made this team have been goaltender Jim Carey, defensemen John Carlson and Scott Stevens, and forwards Nicklas Backstrom and Alexander Ovechkin.

5. While numerous Washington players have been honored with individual awards, their head coaches have also been recognized by voters. The top regular-season head coach receives the Jack Adams Award each season. Bryan Murray won it for 1983-84, Bruce Boudreau took it home for his work in 2007-08, and Barry Trotz captured it for 2015-16.

6. The only Capitals to win more than one major trophy in their career so far have been goaltenders Braden Holtby (2) and Olaf Kolzig (3) along with blueliner Rod Langway (2) and winger Alexander Ovechkin (17). Those who have won an award each are goaltenders Jose Theodore, Jim Carey, Al Jensen, and Pat Riggin and forward Doug Jarvis along with head coaches Barry Trotz, Bruce Boudreau, and Bryan Murray.

7. The highest individual award a player can receive is to be inducted into the Hockey Hall of Fame in Toronto, Canada. Those who are voted into the Hall are done so based on their entire career's worth of work with all teams. So far eight players who have skated with the Capitals at one time or another during their careers have been inducted. These are defensemen Scott Stevens, Rod

Langway, Larry Murphy, and Phil Housley, along with forwards Adam Oates, Sergei Fedorov, Dino Ciccarelli, and Mike Gartner.

8. In total, the Capitals have won 33 major individual NHL awards between 1974 and 2020. They have also won six team awards, for a total of 39. The team awards consist of one Stanley Cup, three President's Trophies, and a pair of Prince of Wales Trophies. The President's Trophy is for the top regular-season team, while the Prince of Wales is given to the winner of the Eastern Conference playoff showdown.

9. Several former Capitals players have been inducted into the United States Hockey Hall of Fame in Eveleth, Minnesota, over the years. These players are defensemen Rod Langway, Kevin Hatcher, Phil Housley, and Ron Wilson, along with forwards Bobby Carpenter and Dave Christian. In addition, former general manager David Poile was inducted in the builder's category. Former Caps player Craig Patrick was also inducted as a non-player for his later work as a coach and general manager.

10. A lesser-known hockey award is the Lester Patrick Trophy. This has been presented by the NHL and USA Hockey since 1966 as a way to honor contributions to the sport in the USA. Those who have served the Capitals in the past and have received the Lester Patrick Trophy are former blueliner Phil Housley and former general manager David Poile.

CONCLUSION

You've just read through some fascinating facts and trivia about the Washington Capitals franchise from their league debut in 1974-75 until the 2019-20 campaign. We hope you found the book entertaining and informative and have perhaps learned a thing or two that you weren't aware of.

Many of the facts may be well known to most fans, but we've also tried to add some more obscure tales and trivia. The main objective of the book is to learn as much about the history of the Washington Capitals, players, coaches, and management as possible and also in the most entertaining manner possible.

We hope you can put this information to good use and will perhaps use it to engage fellow Caps fans in some friendly trivia challenges. You could also share the information with the younger generation of Washington supporters who may not know the team's history as well as others.

It's impossible to list all the odds and ends and facts of the Capitals' history, and there are surely some that aren't included here. But you have a comprehensive starting point if you hope to test the knowledge of fellow Caps fans.

The Washington Capitals are one of the NHL's most

intriguing franchises and a true "rags to riches" story. They've gone from worst to first over the years and are now one of the most consistent clubs in the league. They've lived through some very lean times as well as glorious moments and everything in between. However, they wouldn't be where they are today without you...their passionate and loyal fans.